Observing Children

Second Edition

Books are to
the l

Observing Children

A Practical Guide

Second Edition

Carole Sharman, Wendy Cross
and Diana Vennis

CASSELL
London and New York

Cassell
Wellington House   370 Lexington Avenue
125 Strand   New York
London WC2R 0BB   NY 10017–6550

First published 1995
Reprinted 1996
Second edition 2000

British Library Cataloguing-in-Publication Data
A catalogue record for this book is available from the British Library.

ISBN: 0–304–70627–2 (paperback)

Typeset by York House Typographic Ltd, London
Printed and bound in Great Britain by The Bath Press, Avon

Contents

Preface

This book is intended for use by anyone interested in young children aged from birth to 8 years. Its main aim is to encourage people to enjoy watching children and meeting their needs by observing and recording their development.

It is not linked specifically to any course of study or area of work but, where practical, links are made to the occupational standards written for Early Years Care and Education at NVQ Levels 2 and 3.

The occupational standards contain a complete unit on Observe and Assess the Development and Behaviour of Children – Unit C16. It covers the observation of children aged between 1 and 7 years, and all types of recording techniques can be included in the evidence presented for assessment. Children can be observed either individually or in groups and the observations must cover the physical, intellectual, social and emotional behaviour patterns and interactions in different situations.

By presenting observations as a form of evidence, whether for NVQs or other forms of assessment, you will be demonstrating a detailed knowledge of child development and the principles underlying different types of observations, and the strengths, weaknesses and possible bias in their use.

How to Use the Book

It is intended that the book should be a source of reference which can be referred to throughout your training and beyond. However, if you have not done observations or are unsure of how to undertake them it will be a good idea to work through the book in the order written. The chapters have been designed to lead you through the process and build on knowledge gained earlier. The observations have been highlighted for ease of reference and there are specific activities for you to complete to help you build up your expertise.

Introduction

Watching and listening to their children is a favourite pastime for parents. Some say they 'waste' half a day marvelling at what their young babies can do.

As future carers and educators of children you are probably aware that it is not a waste of time to watch children. This is the way you can learn what stage of development they have reached. Observation will enable you to compare their progress with the expected range for the age group and to plan activities which will lead them forward to the next stage. It will alert you to the needs of the child who has not reached the expected 'norm', or is far ahead of it, so that you can monitor the situation and request the appropriate professional help if required. It will allow you to enjoy each child's unique qualities.

One way of monitoring children's progress would be to study the stages of development and then spend your entire time watching and listening to see if they were reaching the required level. This is obviously not practical nor desirable in the work situation. As professional child carers and educators you will, with practice, be alerted to children's behaviour which gives cause for concern. As learners in the field you need to be equipped with the tools to enable you to make those judgements in an informed way.

The most appropriate way to monitor children's progress, and compare it with what you are learning about the way in which children mature and develop, is to undertake *child observations*. The first aim of this book is to lead you through the process and give you the confidence to be a skilled practitioner.

Chapter 1 discusses in more detail the reasons why we do observations and some of the methods that can be used to record them. It also encourages you to think about children's needs and differing experiences. There is a section (p. 11) which considers the skills you may observe, as one of the main functions of this book is to emphasize the positive aspects of child observations.

Chapter 2 takes you through the stages for recording the written/narrative form of observation and gives you plenty of opportunities to try things for yourself. Chapter 3 gives a more comprehensive guide to the various methods with examples of each, followed by some Aims and Objectives for you to decide on the most appropriate format for recording observations. Chapter 4 reviews the benefits of recording observations in more detail and why the observations are important to the children in your care. In Chapter 5 the ability to link observations to the Desirable Outcomes for Learning is being developed. The ability to use these records and observations to help inform future planning of the curriculum is also discussed. Chapter 6 is divided into developmental areas with suggestions for activities which can be related to the criteria for NVQs. This should help you with ideas for extending children's experience.

Chapter 7 provides a summary of developmental stages which you can refer to; but remember that children will come to you with very different social and cultural experiences. Chapter 7 offers guidelines only.

Observations are part of the curriculum for all child care and education courses. They provide evidence for the portfolios of candidates undertaking NVQs in Early Years Care and Education. They are often viewed with some dismay. The second aim of the book is to make you aware of the value of observations: the difference they can make to your work practice; and that they really can be fun to do.

Look at the picture below and think about what it tells you, read the book and carry out the activities and then look at the picture again. You should have learned a lot more.

Figure I.1 A typical nursery classroom.

Acknowledgements

The authors would like to thank the nursery nurse students of Highbury College for their ideas, and all the nursery and first schools in the Portsmouth area who allowed us to observe and photograph their children.

Thanks also to the parents of the children who gave us permission to use the photographs. All photographs are by Carole Sharman.

1

Why Do Observations?

At the end of this chapter you will be able to answer the
following:

Why do we observe children?
How can we observe them?

'Observations are boring.'
'I can do the observation, but I never know what to say in the
   comments.'
'I find it very difficult to know what to write.'
'It is very hard to watch the children and write at the same time.'
'Why do we have to do observations?'

Above are some of the comments made by nursery nurse students when
asked what they thought of having to do child observations. Below are
some comments made by parents about their children.

'I wonder why he did that?'
'Why can't she understand what I want her to do?'
'He is very naughty, he can't share his toys.'
'She doesn't like to be left for a moment – it is so frustrating.'
'He wants to feed himself, but makes such a mess that I can't let him.'

Students and parents can both learn more about why and when children
do something by having a knowledge of child development, and by
observing what children do. Without that knowledge we can misunder-
stand what they are trying to tell us and this can make life difficult for
everyone.

   All children develop at their own speed. There are genetic and
environmental influences which will affect the rate at which children
develop, but they will broadly follow the same sequence. The way children develop has been studied by many researchers and their results
published in the textbooks you will be using as part of your course of
study. One of the main reasons we observe children, then, is to see if

they are following this general pattern. Observation is an important tool for you to see in practice what you have learned in theory.

Children's development is usually divided into four categories: physical (gross and fine motor skills), intellectual (cognitive), language, social and emotional. (A more detailed account of the areas is given in Chapter 7, pp. 115–19.)

For the purpose of observation it is usual to identify the area you are interested in. This will be stated in your Aims and Objectives of the observation described in detail in Chapter 2.

Before proceeding further it is important for you to review your present understanding of why we carry out observations.

Activity

Without turning back to the Introduction, note down your answers to the following questions:

1. Why do we watch children?
2. What can we see?
3. What can we learn from watching children?
4. How can we help the children through watching them?

We will discuss these questions again at the end of the chapter and you can compare your answers with the suggestions given.

Having decided that observation is a tool which can help with your learning and benefit the children in your care, we need to look at the best ways of carrying out the observations and recording the results.

Here are two important points

1. An observation is like a camera shot, and although it is said that the camera does not lie, it may distort. We should not make judgements about a child on a single observation. We may be alerted to a problem but need to follow it up in order to make an informed conclusion.
2. The very fact that we are carrying out the observation can make a difference to the way the child behaves. He or she may become inhibited or embarrassed, or may play to the audience. Try an experiment: take a camera and a tape recorder into the workplace and see the response when you try to record the 'normal' routine.

If you remember these points then you will be able to make the best use of your observations and also decide which is the best method to use. Researchers will often use video to record children's behaviour so that they can play it back numerous times in order to see in detail the responses. This is particularly true when observing babies, and you have undoubtedly seen the results on television. You may be able to do this, but we are concentrating on the more usual methods of written evidence. The method you choose will normally be dependent on the timescale and what you are hoping to discover.

In the following pages we discuss:

Observation methods
Children's needs and experiences
Skills you may observe.

Observation Methods

Observations can be carried out in many formats, and the examples given here are meant to give you an idea of how some of them can be recorded. We will be discussing all the methods you can employ, their best uses and the exact way to lay out observations in the following chapters.

1. Narrative/free description

This is the style of observation that you will probably start with. It involves watching a child or group of children and noting down what you see. You will need to sit quietly and try to draw as little attention to yourself as possible, remembering that your interaction with the children can affect their behaviour. One way to deter children from talking to you is to avoid eye contact. If they become aware that you are writing, you might say that you are doing some college work.

Written observations usually cover a short period of time. They should be written in the present tense because you are recording things as they happen. Although you will need to set the scene by describing what is going on around, you need to remember that your main focus is the child you are observing.

An example of how you might write is shown on p. 4.

2. Checklists/pre-coded categories

Checklists can be used to record the activities of a single child or a group of children. Unlike the written/narrative observation, which only requires you to write a record of what you see, a checklist needs to be prepared in advance. You will need to consider what you want to find out about the children. Checklist observations are regularly used in schools to record the progress of children. It is important for the teacher to be aware of the needs of the individual child so that programmes can be developed. Most modern classrooms allow the children

Observation

Setting   The home corner in a reception class.

Carl puts on a white gown and a pair of rabbit's ears then starts hopping about. John sits down beside the telephone and then gets up and walks over to the cupboard. He takes out two bowls and puts them onto the floor, then walks over and picks up Carl. He carries Carl over to the bowls and sets him down.

'Eat up, rabbit.'

Carl kneels down and pretends to eat the food. John starts to make 'brrr brrr' noises. He goes over to the telephone, picks it up and listens.

'Auntie is coming to see us.'

Carl appears not to have heard but after a minute he gets up and walks over to the dressing-up box. He takes out a skirt which he puts on over the rabbit outfit. He walks over to John and in a high squeaky voice says: 'Hello, I've come for a visit.'

John looks at Carl and then walks out of the home corner over to the craft table.

a certain amount of freedom to decide their own learning activities so it is essential to keep a record of their achievements. It is important to note here that we are recording a child's *achievements*, not their failure to do something. Of course we may identify a *need* while we are doing so.

An example of a checklist for your group in nursery is shown in Figure 1.1.

N.B. The children may not complete this on one day or in the order given. That does not matter. Also the younger the child, the less likely they are to 'perform to order'. You may obtain a truer picture if you make the assessment into a game.

3. Time sampling/structured description

As the name suggests, this form of recording consists of a series of written records at intervals throughout a period of time. The length of time between the observations, and the length of time you observe for, will depend on the overall timescale for the completed record. This will normally be decided by the reason you are carrying out the observation in the first place. For example, if you want to discover whether a child is

Activity	Sam	Liam	Susan	Shanaz	William
Stands on one leg for three seconds	✓	✓	✓	✓	✕
Jumps in place	✓	✓	✓	✓	✓
Hops on one foot	✕	✕	✓	✕	✓
Kicks ball	✓	✓	✓	✓	✓
Catches large ball	✕	✓	✕	✓	✓
Pedals tricycle	✓	✓	✓	✓	✓

Figure 1.1 Example of checklist.

able to concentrate for the duration of a storytime you might decide to look at that child every minute and record what they are doing. It might look something like this:

Observation

10.01 a.m. Sitting quietly looking at the teacher.

10.02 a.m. Concentrating on the picture being shown to the group.

10.03 a.m. Pulling up her socks and carefully turning over the tops.

10.04 a.m. Responds to her name being called by the teacher.

10.05 a.m. Has her hand up to answer a question which is asked about the story.

. . . and so on.

If a child was aggressive or did not appear to mix very well you might want to observe that child for a morning or even a whole day. In that instance you would probably decide to make the interval 20 minutes or half an hour. Your observation might look something like this:

Observation

9.00 a.m. Comes into class and looks back at mother in the doorway. Spoken to by the class teacher and comes and sits on the floor. Spoken to by another child but does not respond.

9.30 a.m.   Working with a group of six children doing number activities. Asked to pass the pencil container by one of the children – does not respond. Asked again in a louder voice – pushes the container across table but does not make any eye contact.

10.00 a.m. Painting a picture beside another child. Looks across at the other's drawing and stands slightly closer. Approached by teacher.
'What an interesting picture – would you like to tell me what it is?'
Smiles but does not answer.
'Is it a bus?'
Child nods but does not speak.

10.30 a.m. Standing beside the wall in the playground. Moves and goes to stand near the playground duty teacher but does not say anything. Kicks a ball that comes close and walks after it.
'Do you want to play?' asks the child.
Nods and joins in the game, but no speech heard.
. . . and so on.

4. Tracking/structured description

A tracking observation involves following a child for a length of time to discover where they go and what they do. This could be recorded as a written observation but an alternative is to show the result in the form of a diagram. It requires you to draw out the area in which the child will be working in advance. This might be the nursery, classroom or out-door play area. The most obvious use would be to record the activities of a child in the free play time. It would enable you to see if he/she stays with one activity or flits from one to another. You could also use this method to record the number of social contacts a child makes in a given time.

The observation might look like that shown in Figure 1.2.

5. Pie and bar charts/structured description

Pie and bar charts are a useful pictorial way of recording the results of an observation of the whole class. You might want to discover how many children could manage a physical skill like ball catching. You could set up an activity where you threw a ball to the children from a distance of 5 feet. Your record would show how many children caught the ball three times out of three; two times out of three; once out of three; and not at

Figure 1.2 Tracking observation.

all. If your result showed the children had some difficulty with this you might then introduce some activities which give practice in the skill and then repeat the observation. Figure 1.3 on p. 8 shows what the results might look like.

These methods have many uses for collecting information about the children, but they can also be used to give objective evidence about the equipment used in the nursery/classroom/adventure playground, etc. You can watch areas of the setting and note how many times an item is used, e.g. number table, computer, climbing frame. This could give you an opportunity to look at how you would arrange things in the future – or where you might station yourself to give added interest!

Understanding Children's Needs and Experiences

We have discussed various ways of observing and later we will return to them in more detail. One of the reasons identified for doing observations is to meet the *needs* of the children. Children are unique and to be aware of their qualities we need to:

Take an interest in what they are doing.
Listen to what they are saying.

Children may communicate their needs in a variety of individual ways. For instance, one child may scream for attention while a second

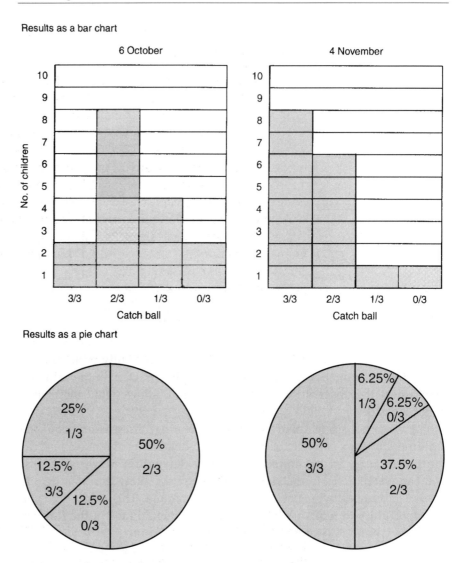

Figure 1.3 Recording results in bar charts and pie charts.

bites another person to express their needs. Both these behaviours are essentially anti-social but we might be able to understand the reason if we observe why it is happening.

Take the example of biting – the observation on p. 9 could help sort out the problem.

Adam will have to learn that it is not a good thing to bite, but he also needs to have someone who will try to understand his problems before he is able to put them into words.

Children always want you to see what they can see, watch with them and enjoy experiences together. A child's excitement is intense when they shout 'Look at me'. If you observe children while they are working instead of just admiring the end product you may be surprised at their

Observation

Adam (20 months) is playing with a ball in the garden. He throws it into the air and then tries to kick it. He moves the ball by walking into it. When it rolls under the chair he chuckles with delight and shouts 'goal!'

Two older children (3 and 4 years) come out of the house to watch. When the ball comes near they pick it up and start to throw it to each other. Adam stands and watches and waits for his turn but they do not include him in the game. The ball rolls towards Adam and he picks it up and hugs it to himself. The 4-year-old walks over and takes it out of Adam's hand and kicks it to the other child. Adam tries to get the ball again but the 3-year-old picks it up, laughs and holds it above her head. As she lowers her arms Adam runs over and bites her hand. She screams and the adults run out to see what has happened. Adam just stands looking bewildered.

'You naughty boy', says his mother.

abilities. For example, a child presents a soggy brown painting to be put in the drying rack. The nursery nurse says: 'I hope it will be dry by going home time'.

When presented with the painting the mother says: 'Very nice dear, what else have you done this morning?'

The following record of an observation demonstrates what the picture was meant to be.

Observation

Dionne (4 years 1 month) puts on an apron and walks over to the painting easel. She picks up the brush from the brown paint pot and draws a circle. She puts two blobs of paint in the circle and returns the brush to the pot. She takes the red brush and paints a curved line at the top of the paper and then puts a line of green below it. She smiles and says: 'A rainbow'.

She stands back for a moment then takes out the yellow brush and draws a sun next to the rainbow.

'Now we need rain.'

[She paints blobs of brown paint onto the picture.]

'It's raining very hard – here's a puddle.'

[She begins to paint lines of brown all over the picture.]

'It's pouring – Grandma is getting very wet.'

[Dionne stands back and looked at the brown picture.]

'I've finished.'

Children are very proud of their achievements, but you must remember that their ability to do something will depend on the amount of practice they have had. We may be tempted to make a judgement quickly from our observation of a child and question their level of development. We must remember *to take into account past experience and environment* before making any assumptions.

If we take the example of riding a bike, for instance, Mary Sheridan (1980) reports: Age 3 years – 'rides tricycle, using pedals, and can steer it round wide corners'.

If a child has a tricyle or attends playschool then that is probably true, but some will not have had that experience. If a child appears to have a delay in any developmental area we should provide activities which enable them to practise the skill before 'testing' their ability.

No one would expect you to take a driving test without having lessons – whatever your age.

To summarize then: *Children need adults to notice their achievements and provide an environment to support their further development.* This can be done by observing a child's progress and assessing their needs in all areas.

Figure 1.4 Examples of ways adults can encourage children in their development.

Figure 1.4 gives some examples of the ways adults can encourage children in their development. You will notice that the areas are linked together as it is inevitable that while you are providing for one, you will also be covering the others. Any activity is likely to include language and hopefully also build self-esteem.

Skills You May Observe

Children need to develop a variety of skills to enable them to fulfil their individual potential. As part of your observations you will need to identify the stage the child has reached so that you can provide experiences to encourage progress. An area that students often find difficult to define is *cognitive* or *intellectual*. Figure 1.5 shows some of the skills involved in the process of learning language and reasoning.

Memory and reasoning allow us to make educated guesses about things we have not directly experienced. The older the child the more he is able to do this. Younger children need to be able to see the problem in order to work it out. This is very obvious when working with numbers – young children need counters or fingers to find the answer but older ones are able to 'do it in their heads'. If you are aware of where the child has reached in their development by observing their skills you will be able to provide activities which will enable them to progress.

Observations linked with progress in skills

Let us consider a child's ability to complete a three-piece jigsaw. Skills developing are:

Physical	Intellectual fine manipulative skills eye–hand co-ordination.
Intellectual	problem solving, concentration, memory concept of size–shape–colour.
Emotional	patience/control frustration/satisfaction.
Social	sharing (with adult or child).
Language	association – pictures and words new words/subjects.

Activity

Try to undertake the following: an observation of a 2-, 3- and 4-year-old each completing the same jigsaws.

1. Make a comparison between the abilities of each child
2. Notice the variation of levels of skills.
3. From your observations devise an action plan to increase the development of skills.

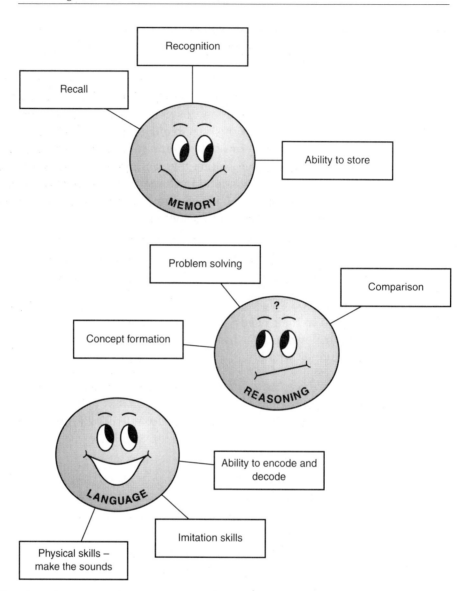

Figure 1.5 Some of the skills involved in memory, reasoning and language.

Observation

For example, Philip (3) can complete a simple three-piece jigsaw. He now insists on placing the pieces upside down on the tray. He is *obviously* trying to find new ways of playing with them.

This is where your role as a facilitator becomes apparent. You can now develop his skills by providing newer/different/more complicated jigsaws to extend his skills and experiences.

Observation

Claire (2) cannot yet complete the jigsaw unaided. She needs an adult beside her to help. She picks up the pieces and puts them at random into the holes – pushing hard to fit them in. When they won't go in she gets frustrated, screws up her face and pushes harder then looks to the adult for help. Adult places hand on top of Claire's and guides the piece into the right place, allowing Claire the final feel of satisfaction when the piece drops into place. She persists in trying again – and each time with the help and patience of an adult she succeeds.

By observing the child and seeing the absorption in the activity you can tell that, although she cannot complete it without help, it is not so difficult that she will not develop the required skills to gain eventual success.

Summary

You have now looked at various observation methods, thought about children's needs and considered some of the skills you may require to encourage and broaden them.

Before we move on to the next chapter, we need to look again at the questions posed at the beginning of this chapter. Some of your answers might include:

1. Why do we watch children? – to discover their unique qualities.

2. What can we see? – what children are able to do;
    how they approach problems and how they
    attempt to solve them;
    children enjoying themselves.

3. What can we learn from watching children? –
    what level they have reached;
    a better understanding of why a child does something;
    reinforce our knowledge of child development;
    try to see things from the child's point of view.

4. How can we help the children through watching them? – by providing activities/resources/support to facilitate these developing skills.

BY WATCHING CHILDREN:
WE EVALUATE THEIR NEEDS
EXTEND THEIR EXPERIENCES
FACILITATE THEIR LEARNING.

2

A Step-by-step Guide to Presenting an Observation

Using the written/narrative style as an example

> At the end of this chapter you will be able to:
>
> Identify aims and objectives.
> Record detailed observations.
> Relate your findings to work practice.

In the previous chapter we outlined some of the usual ways in which observations can be recorded. Now it is your turn to try out the skill. We will begin by looking in detail at how to organize and present an observation using the written/narrative format.

To help you through the stages that will follow we have started with an example of how a completed observation will look, with explanations for the headings used. The **headings in bold type** will actually always remain the same whichever format you use. *An explanation for the headings is given in italics.*

Observation

Observation no. 1 *It is important to number the observations so that you can refer to a particular example if you want to use it as NVQ evidence. It will also demonstrate your progress in an observation file.*

Date 23.6.94 *There are two reasons for recording the date: (1) You may wish to repeat an observation at a later date in order to compare a child's ability with their previous performance; (2) It will enable you to work out the exact age of the child so that you can evaluate your results against the expected developmental stage.*

Time commenced   10.20 a.m.
Time completed   10.30 a.m.   *This allows you to comment more easily on the length of time a child spent on an activity.*

Number of adults 1.
Number of children 4.   *Although you may have decided to observe one child, it is useful to record the number of children in the group as this may have an influence on the behaviour.*

Name of child   Manju.   *It is only necessary to record the first, or a fictitious, name so that the record remains confidential if you are using the observation for study purposes.*

Age   3 years 10 months.   *You will need to know the child's date of birth to work this out. It is important to record the exact age in years and months in order to make a fair comparison with developmental stages.*

Setting   The junk modelling table in the creative area of a nursery school. The children have a free choice of materials but a nursery nurse is available to offer advice if required. *It is not necessary to identify the place by name in order to maintain confidentiality, but it is useful to record the general background to the observation. It is also important to record if an adult is involved, as this is likely to affect the way the children behave.*

Aim   To observe a child who is nearly 4 years old during a junk modelling session in order to identify fine manipulative skills and problem-solving ability. *The Aim of an observation should set out the broad areas of development that you wish to find out.*

Objectives   To observe and record Manju's ability to use scissors and glue spreader. To observe and record Manju's ability to plan her model and work out how to make it. *The Objectives should identify the specific abilities that you wish to observe.*

Record of observation
Manju puts on an apron and approaches the table. She picks up a circular box and turns it over in her hands then puts it back down. She walks round to the other side of the table and selects a larger cereal packet then returns to her original place. She looks at the nursery nurse and smiles.

'What are you going to make?' asks the nursery nurse.

Manju looks at the display on the wall and says: 'A rocket'. She picks up some silver foil and carefully tears it in half. With a well-developed pincer grasp she picks up a glue spreader and dips it into the pot of glue. Some of the glue drips onto the newspaper covering the table as Manju carries the spreader over to her box. The nursery nurse moves the glue pot closer to Manju. Manju tips the glue off her spreader onto the box and smears it over half of one side, then she leans over and puts some more glue onto the spreader and places it on the box. Concentrating very hard, she uses the spreader to cover the whole side. She smiles as she continues to make patterns in the glue.

'Are you going to stick your silver paper on?' asks the nursery nurse.

Manju picks up a piece of the silver paper with her left hand and leans over to put some more glue on the spreader. She holds the paper in the palm of her hand and covers it with glue.

'I think you have enough glue now', says the nursery nurse.

Manju places the piece of glue-covered silver paper onto the box. Her fingers stick to the paper, which lifts off as she attempts to fix it to the box. She looks across at the nursery nurse, who comes over to assist.

'I think you can put the other piece of paper on without any more glue.'

Manju selects a cardboard tube instead. She pushes it against the box and holds it in position for a few moments. When she moves her hand the tube falls off. She picks up the spreader and puts some glue around the end then pushes it down on the box again. As she lets go it falls over.

The nursery nurse picks up another piece of cardboard tube:

'Shall I show you how to fix it?'

Manju nods and watches as the nursery nurse makes a cut about 2 cm long down the side.

'Can you make some more cuts round the edge?'

The nursery nurse hands the scissors to Manju. She manages to put her fingers in them correctly and, holding the tube close to her body, she makes a short cut. She pulls the scissors out and attempts a second incision. The scissors come together at an angle but do not cut.

Manju begins to look anxious. The nursery nurse comes round the table and puts her hand over the scissors to guide them. Together they make several more cuts. The nursery nurse shows Manju how to bend the card back to make a bigger area to glue.

'Now you can stick it to your rocket.'

Manju spreads some glue onto the box and then puts the tube in place. She moves her hand and smiles when it stays in position.

'Do you want to add any more?' asks the nursery nurse.

Manju looks at the model and says: 'No'.
'Shall we put your rocket somewhere safe to dry?'
Manju nods then goes off to wash her hands.

The record should be written as it happens whenever possible. You should concentrate on the areas you are interested in as it will not be possible to record everything the child does.

Conclusion

Manju decided what she wanted to make before she started the model by observing what was on the wall frieze in the creative area. She was able to use the glue spreader and enjoyed putting lots of glue onto the box. She used more than was necessary to stick the paper to it and spent some time making patterns which she appeared to enjoy.

Manju had some difficulty using the scissors but she held them properly. She was not yet able to work out how to fix the cardboard tube to the box, but managed to complete her rocket with the assistance of the nursery nurse.

The conclusion should summarize what you observed and match it to what you hoped to find out – your Objectives.

Evaluation

The developmental milestones for the 4-year-old (p. 134) state that they are 'able to use scissors with practice', and are 'beginning to name drawings before starting'. Manju is not quite 4 but she held the scissors properly and made a partially successful attempt to cut the tube, which is a difficult shape. She was able to name what she planned to do before starting. Manju appears to be operating well within the normal limits for her age.

The evaluation should compare your findings with what you expect for the age group. You should use a recognized source in order to make your comparison. This can be the milestones in Chapter 7 or any other child development book. You can also compare the child with the other children in the class who are the same age.

Recommendations

Continue to offer opportunities for planning her own activities. Encourage activities which will help strengthen fingers (fine manipulative skills), e.g. Play-doh; construction toys.

One of the main uses for your observations is to help children perfect their skills. Some ideas are offered in Chapter 6.

Now that you have seen how a completed observation is set out you should be ready to try the skill for yourself. The following sections have been arranged so that you can work your way through the activities and build on your knowledge.

Activity

1. Discuss with your supervisor or work colleagues the need to undertake an observation. Then decide on a time when you are likely to be interrupted as little as possible.

2. Identify the child that you wish to observe.

3. Sit quietly and record what the child does for five minutes.

   N.B. Refer to the child by first or forename only in order to maintain confidentiality. It is important to stress here that observations carried out as part of your learning are likely to be seen by several people, so it should not be possible to identify the child or the exact location. It will be sufficient to describe the type of surroundings in a general way, e.g. reception class, nursery outdoor play area, indoor swimming pool, etc.

4. When you have finished the observation, read it back to yourself.

You may have found the above activity difficult. It is not easy to record what is taking place as you are trying to watch everything that is happening around you. While you are writing you may miss an important interaction. One way you can speed up your note taking, so that you do not need to have your head down all the time, is to develop a code. This can be quite simple. For example, you may put A→B. This could mean that child A (Ben) went up to child B (Sunil) and exchanged information. This might be very useful if you were recording a child's ability to socialize. You will need to think about possible shortcuts and then note them down, because it is not much use having a lot of observations that you are unable to read back.

This raises another important point about writing up your observations. THE SOONER YOU READ THEM THROUGH AND WRITE THEM OUT FULLY – THE EASIER IT WILL BE. A common excuse made by students who have failed to produce observations for marking is that they have lots 'in rough'. They then have great difficulty in remembering what some of the hasty scribble means. If you write up the observation while it is fresh in your mind you will often be able to visualize the situation again and know what you have written. Ten minutes of your lunch break used in this way can save you a lot of time later on.

Another way to make your recording easier is to identify clearly the reason why you are observing the child and what you hope to find out. This will give you your *Aims* and *Objectives*.

Activity

Figure 2.1 is a picture of two 4-year-olds playing in a sand tray, followed by an account of what took place during a 15-minute observation. (The sand had birdseed mixed in with it.) *Read through* the observation and then *make a list* of what you think it tells you about the children.

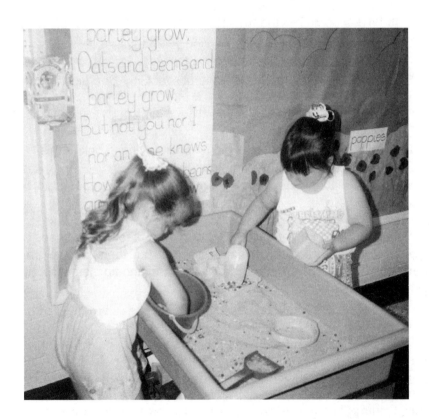

Figure 2.1 Two 4-year-olds playing in a sand tray.

Observation

The children are standing either side of the sand tray running their hands through the sand. Chloe picks up a bowl and begins to fill it up using a large scoop.

Natasha picks up a sieve and fills it with sand. She watches as the sand runs through leaving the seed in the sieve. She picks up a scoop and attempts to use it to move the seed from the sieve to a yogurt pot. Her concentration shows on her face but very little seed goes into the scoop. She leans over to the tray of utensils and selects a spoon which she uses to carefully transfer the seed. After six spoonfuls she tips the rest of the seed into the pot allowing it to spill over the sides back into the tray. She puts down the sieve, picks up the scoop and moves round to the other side of the table.

Chloe: 'This is my side.'

She looks round but there are no adults looking. She picks up the sieve.

Natasha takes it from her saying: 'That's mine' and walks back to her own side.

Chloe fills a dish and turns to the teacher saying: 'Look at this.'

Ryan walks up to the tray and starts to dig.

Natasha: 'Teacher . . . there's three, there's only supposed to be two.'

Ryan walks away.

Natasha: 'Shall we get all the toys out and collect all the seeds?'

She starts to collect all the utensils and put them on the tray, watched by Chloe. She starts to sieve the sand and tip the seeds into a corner of the tray.

'We'll just have seeds shall we?'

Chloe picks up a sieve and begins to do the same.

Natasha: 'I'm going to nanny's house for lunch – no dinner.'

Chloe: 'I've got some more seeds for you.'

They pick up individual seeds using a pincer grasp for about two minutes.

Natasha puts some seeds in a pot and brings them over to me: 'Here is a cake for you.'

We talk about the cake.

A child who is deaf comes up to me and attracts my attention by rubbing my cheek. He indicates that he wants to play in the sand.

Chloe looks across and says: 'NO, Natasha is still here.'

Natasha returns to the sand then brings back another pot of seed with a lid on.

> Chloe walks over to me and says: 'You know what? I've got a C.H.L.O.E. in my name.'
>
> Natasha offers me the pot of seeds: 'I've made a big cake...no I'll open it as it's full up.'
>
> The children walk back to the sand but teacher announces that it is clear-up time.

When you have completed your list of comments about the children, compare it with the suggestions given at the end of the chapter (p. 32). Try not to look too soon. You will notice that the list has been arranged into different areas of development. If you try to think in these terms you will probably find it easier to identify areas you wish to observe.

So now you have several reasons for observing these children. However, if you focus on *one* area of development you can look and record in more detail. Go back and look at the observation again. You can see that although there is a lot happening, there are also a lot of gaps. Unless you were looking for social interaction it would probably be better to concentrate on one child and look at one area of development – e.g. language, intellectual/cognitive skills, fine manipulative skills, imaginative play. (See Chapter 7 for more details of developmental areas.)

Activity

Figures 2.2 to 2.6 show children aged from about 3 to 6½ years in various activities.

In each situation, choose to observe either a single child or the whole group, then suggest what you might want to find out. Try to formulate specific Aims and Objectives, but if you find this difficult discuss your ideas with your tutor before you decide how to proceed.

Handy tip If you are stuck for ideas try looking at the section on developmental milestones in Chapter 7, or any child development book, and see what children are expected to do at the various ages. This should help you formulate your ideas for Aims and Objectives.

Remember, *Aims* and *Objectives* are just the formal way of setting out your plan to discover what children are able to do. For example, your *Aim* could be to observe a teacher talking to a child. Your *Objectives* could be to discover if the child listened to what was being said and if they could understand what was being asked. This would be written as:

Aim   To observe the class teacher communicating with a 4-year-old.
Objectives   1. To identify the child's ability to listen to a simple request.
2. To identify the child's ability to carry out a simple request.

Your aim could be to observe a child (in a group) at lunch time to see how the child behaves. This could be written as:

Aim   To observe a 5-year-old using social skills when sitting at the lunch table.
Objectives   1. To identify the child's ability to respond to others. 2. To identify the child's ability to use cutlery effectively.

Or your aim could be to discover how good children's physical abilities are. This could be used to identify very specific skills and be written as:

Aim   To observe the gross motor skills of a group of 3- to 4-year-olds during an outdoor activity session.
Objectives   To identify and record the children's ability to:

      jump on the spot;
      hop on one foot;
      kick a ball;
      catch a large ball;
      pedal a tricycle.

N.B. These would be suitable Aims and Objectives for the checklist example given in Chapter 1 (p. 5) and the photograph of the children shown in Figure 2.5.

Figure 2.2

Figure 2.3

Activity

Now that you have successfully formulated a variety of Aims and Objectives for the children in the photographs, it is time to try out the technique in your own practical placement. You might try out one of the examples identified in the previous activity or construct some new ones of your own. You will have noticed that the Aim often refers to the age of the child so it will be important to record the exact age in years and months. Your Objectives for a child who is just 3 years are unlikely to be the same as for a child who is 3 years and 11 months.

In the first instance it might be a good idea to think of an observation in each of the areas of development. So for the age group you have chosen write out an *Aim* and *Objectives* for:

fine motor skills
gross motor skills

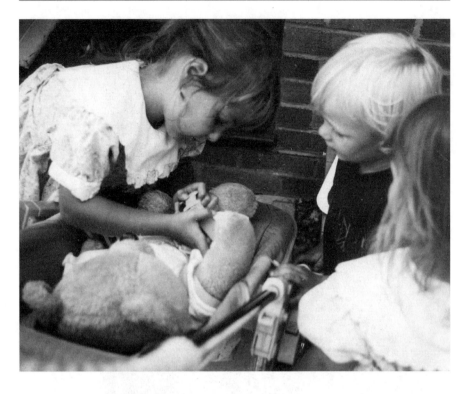

Figure 2.4

intellectual/cognitive development
language development
social skills
emotional development.
(Refer to Chapter 7 if you need help in identifying the areas of development.)

You will now need to decide whether you can find out these things by observing the child during the normal daily routine or whether you need to introduce a specific activity in order to achieve your objective.

When you have planned your observations, discuss them with your supervisor to make sure they will be possible in the framework of the nursery or classroom routine. There are many pre-set goals to be met, especially those laid down by the National Curriculum, so it may not always be convenient for you to introduce some of your ideas. However, a compromise is usually possible.

Having established what you are going to do, set aside convenient time and begin to record your observations.

Figure 2.5

You will now have a collection of observations which focus on an area of development. The next step is to look at what use you can make of them.

The first thing you need to consider is whether the Objectives have been met. This is discussed in the *Conclusion* by looking again at what you have observed and matching it to what you hoped to find out.

There follows an example of an observation with a Conclusion. The format also includes details of the child, such as name and age, and details of the setting. We have also noted the time the observation started and finished.

Observation

Name of child   Susan   **Age**   9 months
                                   Time commenced   5.15 p.m.
                                   Time completed   5.25 p.m.

Setting   The bathroom of the family home.

Aim   To observe a 9-month-old baby during bathing.

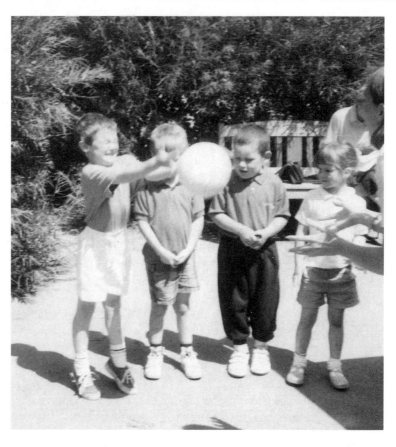

Figure 2.6

Objectives   To identify and record the child's physical skills.
To identify and record the child's interaction with the
adult carer.

Record of observation

The nanny lays Susan on a towel on the floor and starts to undress
her. Susan concentrates on the adult face and appears to be listening to her as she explains what she is doing.

'Let's take this jumper off, shall we?'

The nanny pulls the jumper over Susan's head and says 'Boo!'
Susan squeals with delight. She lies quite still as the nanny unfastens
the dungarees and pulls them off, then removes the vest.

Susan starts to wriggle and attempts to roll over. The nanny gives
her a rattle which gains her attention and she lies quite still, holding it
in front of her while the nappy is removed.

As she is lifted into the bath she drops the rattle onto the floor.
Once in the bath Susan picks up the sponge and puts it in her mouth.
She begins to suck it and splutters in surprise as the water goes
down her throat. She turns and moves onto her knees and grasps the

handle on the side of the bath. She pulls herself up into the standing position and leans over the edge. The nanny sits her down in the water again and gives her a plastic book to look at. Susan passes the book from one hand to the other and then puts it in her mouth. She drops it into the water and looks around for something else. The nanny fills a plastic bottle by pushing it under the water. Susan watches the bubbles and laughs, then begins to shout 'da-da-da'.

'Is daddy coming home soon?'

Susan begins to grizzle and rub her eyes, so nanny quickly finishes washing her and then puts out her hands. Susan holds up her arms to be lifted out.

Conclusion

Susan was very mobile during the observation. She wanted to roll over when she was on the floor and she pulled herself up in the bath. She was able to hold an object in her hand and pass it into the other hand.

Susan responded to the language used and joined in the game of Peek-a-boo. She co-operated by lifting her arms when it was time to come out of the bath.

You can see how the Conclusion summarizes what you have observed and relates the findings to the Objectives.

Activity

Look back at the previous activity and write Conclusions for your own observation.

This activity almost completes what you should include in a written/ narrative observation. You now need to consider how observations can help your work practice by reinforcing your knowledge of child development, and help the children in your care by identifying experiences which will lead them forward.

The value of observations is in their use, not just for a collection in a file. We make use of the observation by evaluating it, comparing it to the expected developmental stage and then making any recommendations. It is possible to compare the development with the other children of a similar age, but it is more usual to refer to a recognized source.

For example:

Observation

Names of children   Martin   **Age**   5 years 2 months
                         Lily   5 years 4 months
                                          Time commenced   3.10 p.m.
                                          Time completed   3.25 p.m.

Setting   Distribution of Christmas presents in the reception class.

Aim   To observe the behaviour of two 5-year-olds when given their presents.

Objectives   To identify and record the reactions of the children.
                  To identify and record any language.

Record of observation

Martin is the first child to be given a parcel. He thanks the teacher and puts it on the floor next to him. He picks at the tape around the parcel with his right hand and carefully folds back the paper using both hands. He picks up the present and waves it over the children's heads.

Martin (to nursery nurse): 'Look what I've got Miss. It's a colouring book.'

Nursery nurse: 'It's beautiful, Martin.'

Martin carries it over to where Lily is sitting unwrapping her book.

Lily: 'What's your picture?'

Martin: 'The same as yours.'

Lily: 'My book's red.'

Martin: 'Mine's blue.'

Lily: 'They're different.'

She rubs the book with her hand.

Martin takes the colouring book over to the table and wraps it in the paper again. He picks up the parcel but it falls to pieces. He lays the book on the table and folds the paper around it again, trying to restick the used tape. The teacher says it is time to get ready to go home. Martin leaves the book on the table and runs to collect his coat and school bag. He picks up his coat and puts his hood on his head and then puts his arms in the sleeves. He walks over to the table with his bag and puts the present inside. He puts the bag straps over his head and onto his shoulder and then goes and sits on the carpet.

Teacher: 'Where's your colouring book Martin?'

Martin: 'It's in my bag, so it won't get wet.'

Conclusion

Martin was excited with his present and was anxious to show it to an adult and a special friend. He showed a caring attitude by attempting to rewrap it and then putting it away in his school bag.

Both children were able to identify the colours red and blue and to notice the difference between the two.

Evaluation

According to Mary Sheridan (1980) the 5-year-old names four primary colours and matches ten or twelve. Both children recognized red and blue.

The children were aware that there was a difference in colour. Valda Reynolds (1994) refers to the work of the Swiss psychologist Jean Piaget who described the five main stages of cognitive development. In the Intuitive period, 4 to 7 years, children 'begin to associate objects with each other and to be aware of differences'.

Both children appear to be operating within the normal limits for their age.

Recommendation

Continue to offer opportunities for sorting, matching and sequencing.

Activity

You can now complete your own observations by making the final evaluation. Look at your *Aims* and *Objectives*, read through your observations and make sure you have summarized them in the *Conclusion*. Look at the *Stage/Level of normal development* for the age group and make a *Comparison* with your findings. The previous example refers to stages described in books you will find listed in the bibliography, but you can use the milestones given in Chapter 7.

Points to remember
- Be specific in your comments.
- Do not make sweeping statements or assumptions about a child.
- Try always to be objective in your findings.

Finally, you should make any recommendations for further observation or activities. In order to give you some ideas for progression in developmental areas we have included a few examples in Chapter 6. No doubt you will be able to think of many more.

The exercises you have accomplished should have enabled you to complete your structured written/narrative observations – that is, observations which have been planned to discover the abilities of a child or children in a certain developmental area: observations which have predetermined Aims and Objectives. Once you have been recording these for a while and discovered their value you may want to use them to note language or behaviour which just happens around you. This would mean writing without specifically formulated Objectives although it is likely that what interested you was related to one area of development. This would be called an *unplanned* or *unstructured* written/narrative observation. In fact although it was unplanned it should have a structure. The format should still include details of the child so that conclusions, evaluations and recommendations can be made.

For example:

Observation

Name of child   Sean
Age of child   4 years 1 month   **Time commenced**   1.45 p.m.
                                        Time completed   2.15 p.m.

Setting   The water tray in the outside play area of a nursery.

Record of observation
Sean has a boat in his right hand which he propels through the water. He makes the noise of an engine as he pushes it along. He lifts it out and watches as the water runs out of it then pushes it down the chute several times using both right and left hands.

Sean continues to play quietly and with concentrated effort. He pushes the boat round the edge of the tray and then towards the island in the middle. He talks quietly to himself and makes engine noises. He picks up some plastic people from the edge of the trough and puts them in the water, then splashes them.

Nursery nurse: 'Are they having a bath or a swim?'
Sean: 'A swim.'
    Sean picks up a plastic mermaid and pushes it through the water.
Nursery nurse: 'Is she going swimming again?'
Sean: 'Yes, she's going like that.'
    He skims her across the water. 'I'm warmer now with my hands in the water.'

Sean continues to play with the mermaid. He talks to himself rather than the nursery nurse: 'When she went, she had yellow seaweed in her hair. She fell down in the sea.'

Sean puts a figure in the boat and then starts to splash so the boat rocks up and down and the figures fall out.

Nursery nurse: 'Who's splashing the water? We've lost the prince.'

Sean throws all the people into the water.

Nursery nurse: 'Did you find the prince?'

Sean: 'He was sitting on the island. He's lying on the beach now – he's tired. They are splashing on the island and they are fed up with this.'

The nursery nurse moves away. A group of other children come to play in the water but Sean does not take much notice of what they are doing. He splashes the water onto his face and then puts the people back into the boat. Most of the other children move away but Scott picks up some of the people from beside the water and comes to join Sean.

Sean: 'You'll have to walk round there with your people. You haven't got a tail, I'm a mermaid.'

Scott: 'I'm a mermaid as well.'

Sean: 'That's my sea. Your sea is over there.'

He picks up the figures and gives them a shake: 'You are naughty people.' He turns to Scott: 'She's pretending she doesn't want to marry him.' He assumes the role of the prince and says: 'What am I going to do?'

He picks up the mermaid and throws her into the water. He now assumes her role: 'You're not going to get me because I'm a mermaid.'

The nursery teacher announces that it is snack time. Sean goes on playing for a few minutes and then puts down the figures and walks towards the door.

Conclusion

Sean had been playing in the water for several minutes when the observation started. I was interested to see how long his concentration span would last and what language he was using. He played in the water for half an hour. Several children came and went during this time but Sean did not take much notice of them. He did interact with Scott when he joined in the game.

Sean kept up a running commentary during his imaginative play. He had obviously seen the video of the Little Mermaid story and became very absorbed in acting it out. His language was grammatically correct.

Evaluation
According to the developmental milestones collated in Chapter 7 – 'Dramatic make-believe play can be sustained for long periods' by the 4-year-old, and 'Speech is intelligible and essentially grammatically correct' – Sean appears to operate well within the range of expected behaviour.

Recommendations
Continue to offer opportunities for imaginative play. Encourage Sean to record his play by telling the other children at recall time, or drawing a picture.

You have therefore made use of your observation even though you had no set objectives at the outset. It cannot be stressed too often that observations are tools to be used to assist your learning and provide a basis for planning children's progression.

You should now be ready to move on to other forms of recording. These will be discussed in the next chapter.

Suggestions for answers to the second 'Activity'

Some of the things you might have learned about Chloe by reading the observation are:

Physical
Good fine manipulative skills – pincer grasp.
Good eye–hand co-ordination using implements.

Intellectual
Good concentration.
Understands concept of number.
Understands mimed gestures.
Shows imaginative skills – seeds in the pot become a cake.
Can spell out the letters of own name.
Language essentially correct in pronunciation and tense.

Social
Works well with others to collect seed.

Emotional
Quite stable and independent.
Not very willing to share.
Still likes the attention of an adult.

3

Experimenting with Observational Techniques

At the end of this chapter you will be able to:

Record in a variety of ways.
Recognize the strengths and weaknesses of the methods.

Now that you have mastered the art of observing and interpreting the content of the observation in the written/narrative form, it is time to begin looking at the variety of other methods in more detail. You are fortunate as a child carer and educator to have the opportunity to use a wide range of methods, and to gain a realistic awareness of the strengths and weaknesses of each method.

Figure 3.1 shows four methods which can be used: diagrammatic, sampling, written and checklists. You should from this be able to see the learning which can be achieved by recording children's behaviour in a structured way. Whichever method is chosen to record the observation, however, it must be remembered that each one will need to include the same preliminary information, evaluation and conclusion as in the written/narrative form. There must always be a reason for undertaking the observation. Once completed you must make evaluation and recommendations. Remember that your evaluation should be based on your knowledge of child development and that you should never be judgemental. If you are in any doubt about what children should be able to do at a certain age, then refer to the milestones in Chapter 7: 'Developmental Milestones from Birth to 8 Years'. However, remember that children of the same age may have had different experiences and be at different stages. Your recommendations should be for the benefit of the child – you are looking at what that child *can do* and then building on that. If you feel that you have not achieved what you set out to discover then you may need to try one of the other methods.

Figure 3.1 sets out some of the types of observation which are commonly used. You will see that the examples build on the information given in Chapter 1. There follow some suggestions for when you might use the different types of recording techniques.

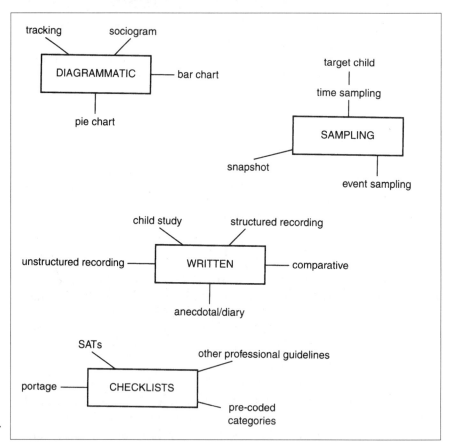

Figure 3.1 Types of observational techniques.

Diagrammatic

Tracking: Observing and recording a child's or children's movements around a limited area for a length of time, e.g. classroom, nursery or garden.

Sociogram: Observing and recording children's social behaviour by plotting their interactions or compiling a graph of their expressed friend-ships.

Bar/block chart: A pictorial method of recording an observation of a whole class's ability to undertake a specific task. A way of showing blocks of time spent on an activity.

Pie chart: An alternative method of recording a time sampling obser-vation or bar chart.

Sampling

Time sampling: Observing and recording what a child is doing every minute for a limited period, e.g. 15 minutes, or at intervals during a set period of time, e.g. every 15 minutes over a morning or afternoon.

Event sampling: Observing and recording certain events as they occur, e.g. aggressive behaviour or temper tantrums.

Snapshot: Observing and recording events at a particular moment. Useful for comparison or to monitor use of equipment or a specific play area.

Written

Structured recording: Observing and recording for a specific reason, e.g. capabilities of a child on entry to school, or ability to do a specific task, e.g. draw a person.

Unstructured recording: Observing a child or children without a pre-determined aim. This type of observation is spontaneous and usually comes about as a result of something interesting or unexpected happening. It may be more difficult to evaluate but could provide you with recommendations for further planned observation. It is a reason for keeping a small notebook and pencil in your pocket.

Comparative: Observing two children and comparing their abilities. Observing one child at intervals and evaluating progress.

Child study: Observing a child over a period of time to evaluate their overall developmental progress. This usually includes some details of the child's background and always requires the parents' permission.

Anecdotal/diary: A record of a child over a period of time which consists of a series of unstructured observations.

Checklists

Observing and recording specific aspects of a child's development using a pre-coded checklist of developmental milestones. This is often undertaken when children first enter school to see what they are able to do. It is also commonly used when working with special needs children to monitor their progress. Portage is a checklist which breaks down the milestones into smaller steps which are used to develop a plan for the parents and carers to work with the child.

SATs are checklists of attainment which are set by government in England and Wales to monitor children's progress. Other countries and agencies have similar systems on which to base their educational or social targets.

You might also consider using different media to help you record your observation, but this should always be discussed with your supervisor in the interest of confidentiality, as film or tape will obviously make the child and setting more obvious.

Figure 3.2 below shows you some of the different recording media you might use.

It is not possible to demonstrate the use of video or tape in this book, but the following examples are written in different formats for you to use as reference. At the end of the chapter there are some suggested Aims and Objectives for you to decide which method would be most suitable to enable you to assess the abilities of the child or children you are observing.

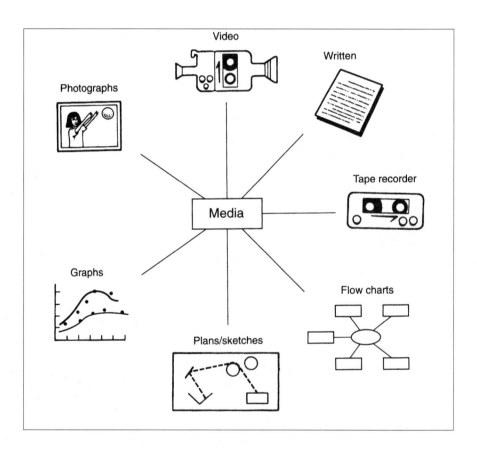

Figure 3.2 Different media for recording observation.

Diagrammatic

Tracking

As stated in Chapter 1, the usual reason for undertaking a tracking observation is to record the time a child spends with an activity or the number of activities they choose. The following example illustrates its use to track a child to discover motor skills on a choice of apparatus. Before commencing, you will need to draw a plan of the area that you are going to observe the child in. You will need to consider how you are going to record the movement, e.g. do you need to devise a code? You will also need to think about your Objectives and how they can be met. In the example in Chapter 1 (p. 7), the Objectives were likely to have been connected to the time the child spent on the activity, so it was important to note times on the diagram. In the following example you will see that the principal objective is to discover which apparatus is chosen. You do not, therefore, need to note time. However, there is a second Objective: to identify the skills used on the apparatus. There is not usually space on the diagram to write this, especially if you identify any difficulties. You will therefore need to note this down separately.

Observation

Date of observation   22.3.94   **Time commenced**   10.50 a.m.
                                      Time completed   11.05 a.m.

Number of children   Whole class

Number of adults   2

Name of child   Adrian   **Age**   6 years exactly

Aim   To observe a 6-year-old while in a formally arranged setting of the gymnastic apparatus in the school hall.

Objectives   To track the choice of apparatus used.
                 To identify and record Adrian's gross motor skills whilst using apparatus.

Setting   The school hall set out for a PE lesson to be used by the whole class.

Record of observation
Ropes   Some difficulty climbing onto the end of the rope and not able to swing successfully, but spends several minutes trying.

Hoops, balances, horse   Not used.

Climbing frame   Most time spent here. Climbs quite well initially but rather hesitant near the top of the frame. Descending is rather a problem. Adrian feels carefully for each rung before moving.

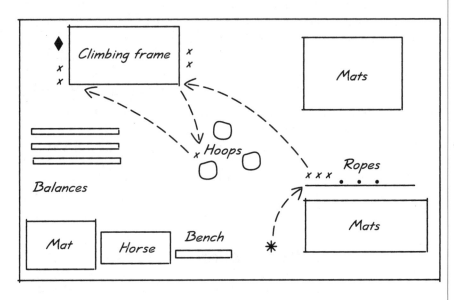

Code

✱   Start
◆   Finish
– –→ Moving between apparatus
x x x Working on apparatus

Figure 3.3 Tracking observation.

Conclusion

From the tracking observation it is obvious that Adrian prefers to work on the large apparatus – either the climbing frame or the ropes, and avoiding the balances and horse. Adrian found difficulty in climbing onto the knot of the rope and then swinging. On the climbing frame he moved alternate arms and legs, reaching up above his head with arms extended and carefully watching where he was going. However, he appeared hesitant and apprehensive when near the top of the frame. The higher he climbed, the less fluent were his movements and he stopped several times to watch other children. He climbed down apprehensively, feeling for each rung before making a move.

Evaluation

According to Catherine Lee (1990, p. 186), a typical 6-year-old 'enjoys using large apparatus for climbing, swinging by arms, hanging by knees. Can somersault, skip with a rope, run and jump and use climbing ropes.' Although Adrian is keen to participate in these activities and likes to use the large apparatus, he has not yet gained confidence, and is unable to move fluently as most children of this age would be able to do. Most children enjoyed the vigorous physical play and used their bodies confidently and actively. Adrian appeared hesitant and apprehensive and enjoyed activities that he had some success with and returned to these, unlike most 6-year-olds, who are keen to master new skills and practise until they perfect them.

Recommendations

Adrian needs more activities to gain self-confidence. He also needs more practice in physical activities and should be encouraged to participate in all the apparatus work and free-standing activities.

This record shows very clearly the value of observing children as individuals. In the general rush of the class activity it is easy to miss the fact that one child is having some difficulty. Experienced workers will usually spot that a child needs some extra help, but it is always useful to have recorded proof.

Sociogram

The sociogram records the social contacts a single child makes, or the friendships among a group of children. It is interesting to do but is subject to considerable distortion. A child who is generally very outgoing may have a day when they are happy to play by themselves for most of the time. Young children make and break friendships very quickly. These things should be remembered when drawing up conclusions.

There are several ways that you can record a sociogram. For the single child, time sampling (pp. 4–6) or tracking are probably the best. This will show you how many contacts a child makes during a set period of time. For the group situation, one possibility is to use the snapshot method (p. 57) and record who children are playing with at a certain time. Playtime is usually best as children are more likely to choose their companions during a free play session. The alternative is to ask children to draw, write or tell you about their friendships.

Observation

Group sociogram of friendships

Date 6.6.93

Number of children Whole class   **Ages**   5 years 10 months to 6 years 7 months.

Setting A first school, year 1, in a classroom.

Aim To discover the friendship groups in the class.

Objectives To discover if boys and girls mix in their friendships. To record if some children are more popular.

Record of observation

Each child was questioned individually and asked to name their three best friends. Figure 3.4 shows the results; all the children in the class are included. The names on the vertical axis were chosen by those in the boxes beside them.

Conclusion

All the boys chose same-sex friends, as did most of the girls. The only exceptions were Ruth, who named James P, and Karen, who chose her twin brother Joshua, and Michael. It was interesting to note that Michael was also one of her brother's choices.

Adam C, James P, Matthew, Katie and Elizabeth were among the most popular children. A large number of children chose each other as friends. Four children were not chosen by any of the other children.

Evaluation

The majority of the results were as anticipated as I have been with the class for two and a half terms and know the children quite well.

The group tended to choose children of the same sex. This has been noted by Valda Reynolds (1994): 'By the age of 7 to 8 the child will be very much aware of sexual differences. Boys of this age usually prefer to be involved in traditional masculine games and activities, keeping mainly in the company of boys. Girls likewise tend to keep to their own sex, although they are rather more flexible than boys.'

The children chosen most often tend to be outgoing and make friends quite easily. I was surprised that Jade was chosen so often as she can be rather aggressive at times. Most of the children who named her are fairly quiet and perhaps need a dominant character to motivate them.

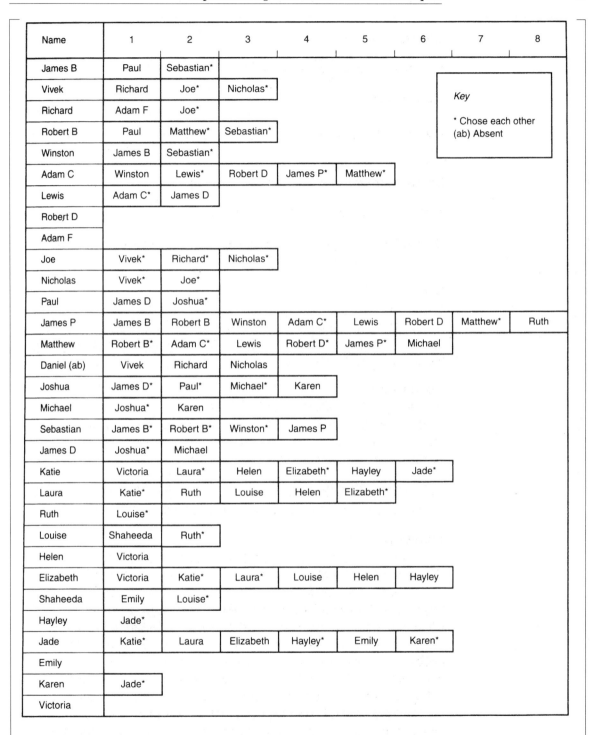

Name	1	2	3	4	5	6	7	8
James B	Paul	Sebastian*						
Vivek	Richard	Joe*	Nicholas*					
Richard	Adam F	Joe*						
Robert B	Paul	Matthew*	Sebastian*					
Winston	James B	Sebastian*						
Adam C	Winston	Lewis*	Robert D	James P*	Matthew*			
Lewis	Adam C*	James D						
Robert D								
Adam F								
Joe	Vivek*	Richard*	Nicholas*					
Nicholas	Vivek*	Joe*						
Paul	James D	Joshua*						
James P	James B	Robert B	Winston	Adam C*	Lewis	Robert D	Matthew*	Ruth
Matthew	Robert B*	Adam C*	Lewis	Robert D*	James P*	Michael		
Daniel (ab)	Vivek	Richard	Nicholas					
Joshua	James D*	Paul*	Michael*	Karen				
Michael	Joshua*	Karen						
Sebastian	James B*	Robert B*	Winston*	James P				
James D	Joshua*	Michael						
Katie	Victoria	Laura*	Helen	Elizabeth*	Hayley	Jade*		
Laura	Katie*	Ruth	Louise	Helen	Elizabeth*			
Ruth	Louise*							
Louise	Shaheeda	Ruth*						
Helen	Victoria							
Elizabeth	Victoria	Katie*	Laura*	Louise	Helen	Hayley		
Shaheeda	Emily	Louise*						
Hayley	Jade*							
Jade	Katie*	Laura	Elizabeth	Hayley*	Emily	Karen*		
Emily								
Karen	Jade*							
Victoria								

Key

* Chose each other
(ab) Absent

Figure 3.4 Record of observation.

The fact that a large number of children chose each other is characteristic of 5- and 6-year-olds according to Brain and Martin (1989) who say: 'Children of this age are often happiest in pairs'.

Of the children who polled no votes Robert D and Adam F are quiet and seem to prefer playing on their own, and Emily can be rather bossy. Victoria's result was rather surprising but she is due to move soon, so this could be a reason.

Recommendations

Although the results were much as expected it would be a good idea to repeat the observation at a later date to see if the same friendship groups exist. However, the results appear sufficiently accurate to use as a guide for the class teacher when considering next year's class list, as the class is due to be split.

Bar chart

In Chapter 1 we looked at the bar chart as a method of recording a class's ability to complete a task. In the following example, the bar chart is used to give a pictorial representation of the time spent on different activities during a typical day's routine for twins. The times are recorded throughout the day and then transferred to the chart.

Observation

Date of observation   14.9.93   **Time commenced**   9.00 a.m.

                                         Time completed   4.30 p.m.

Number of adults   2

Number of children   2

Names of children	Aidan	**Age**	1 year 2 months
	Marc		1 year 2 months

Setting   Throughout the house.

Aim   To observe the care plan of 1-year-old twins throughout the day.

Objective   To record in minutes the amount of time spent on social care and play on a typical day.

Record of observation

9.00 – 9.10 a.m.	Play in the playroom.
9.10 – 9.15 a.m.	Nappy change.
9.15 – 9.30 a.m.	Play in the playroom.
9.30 – 9.40 a.m.	Snack time.
9.40 – 10.15 a.m.	Play in the playroom.
10.15 –10.30 a.m.	Face washing and dressing for outdoors.
10.30 – 12 noon	Outing to the park.
12 noon – 12.15 p.m.	Watch TV.
12.15 – 12.45 p.m.	Lunch.
12.45 – 1.10 p.m.	Garden play.
1.10 – 1.20 p.m.	Wash and nappy change.
1.20 – 3.05 p.m.	Sleep and rest.
3.05 – 3.10 p.m.	Nappy change.
3.10 – 3.20 p.m.	Play in the playroom.
3.20 – 3.30 p.m.	Snack time.
3.30 – 4.30 p.m.	Play in the playroom.

Conclusion

The majority of the twins' day consisted of playtime and outings – 250 minutes. Children of this age still require a daytime sleep – 105 minutes. Apart from a short period watching TV, the rest of the day was taken up by washing and feeding – 85 minutes.

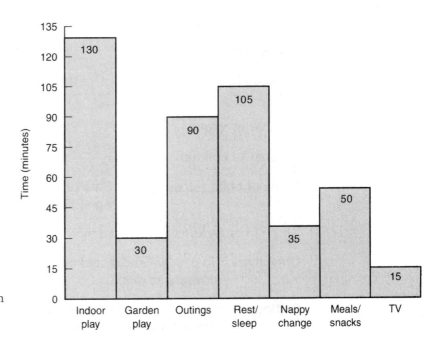

Figure 3.5 Bar graph showing time spent on each activity throughout the day.

Evaluation

The day care programme followed by this family is very similar to one recommended by Patricia Geraghty (1988), who states in the section about planning a child's day: 'The core of the programme for the young child in day care is play, balanced by regular times allotted for routines such as washing, lunch, snacks and a rest period.'

Recommendations

In order to evaluate the quality of the children's daily routine some detailed written/narrative observations of the play should be carried out.

Pie chart

Pie charts are a pictorial way of showing a period of time or a number of children divided up into percentages of a circle (360 degrees). It would be possible to show the bar graph in the previous example in a pie chart format.

In Chapter 1 we looked at pie charts as a way of illustrating percentages of the class who could carry out a procedure. In this example we are using the chart to show the amount of time a child spends on different activities. This can cover any length of time, but it is likely that the younger the child, the shorter the time, as younger children are more liable to have a shorter attention span for one activity.

Observation

Date of observation   7.3.94   **Time commenced**   10.45 a.m.
                                        Time completed   11.00 a.m.

Number of adults   1

Number of children   3

Name of child   Joseph   **Date of birth** 21.10.90
                                  Age   3 years, 6 months

Aim   To observe a 3½-year-old during a free-choice session.

Objectives   To observe and record his concentration span at different activities.

Setting   In the quiet area of the nursery which had been set out with various activities.

Record of observation

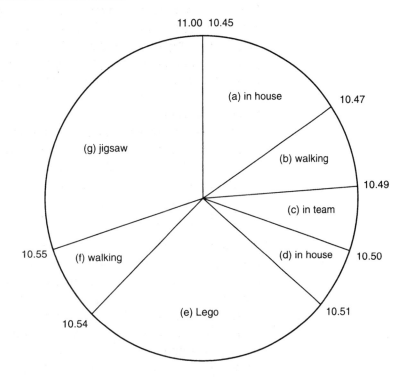

11.00 10.45

(a) in house

10.47

(g) jigsaw

(b) walking

10.49

(c) in team

10.55

(f) walking

(d) in house 10.50

(e) Lego

10.51

10.54

Figure 3.6 Pie chart showing percentage of time on each activity.

(a) Joseph kneels down and moves the ladder in and out of the doll's house. Using his right hand for the majority of the time, he brings the ladder in and out of the house, bending over as he tries to put the ladder back into the house. Carefully watching what he is doing, he puts down the ladder and picks up a piece of furniture with his right hand, rubs his fingers around the furniture without looking at it, and puts it down on the floor beside him. He stands up.

(b–c) Joseph walks aimlessly around the room and finally stops at the Lego. He puts both hands into the Lego box and moves the bricks around, while watching Daniel who has moved to the doll's house. Joseph moves over towards the train set and crouches down, watching Matthew pushing a train along. He stands up and steps over the railway track, then turns towards the doll's house.

(d) Joseph kneels and picks up the ladder with his right hand. He bends over and carefully places the ladder midway between the first and ground floor of the house. He moves around the doll's house on his knees, and when almost completely around the house he stands up and moves back to the Lego table.

(e) Joseph stands by the side of the Lego table and picks up a small piece using the thumb and finger of his right hand. He puts it onto the table and pushes it down using the same two fingers. He repeats this three more times before moving away from the table.

(f)   Joseph walks round the room without taking much notice of what is laid out on the various tables. The nursery nurse suggests that he might like to do a jigsaw puzzle and he answers: 'Yes' and walks over to the table.

(g)   Joseph sits down at the jigsaw table with the nursery nurse. He removes the pieces from the puzzle board, using his thumb and index finger. He begins to put the pieces back into the correct spaces. He does not need help but looks to the nursery nurse for encouragement at intervals. He completes the puzzle and smiles.

Conclusion

When given a free choice of activities Joseph took some time in choosing, and even when he settled to an activity it could not hold his attention span for longer than a few minutes, after which he would get up and walk around the room before stopping briefly to play with another activity. With the help of an adult Joseph found it easier to settle and concentrate.

Evaluation

Joseph has been attending nursery for only half a term and is still overwhelmed by the wide choice of activities available. After he was offered guidance and felt reassured, he sat and concentrated well. Having been in nursery for such a short time he is just beginning to explore the nursery environment, and prefers to stand and watch other children rather than join in himself. He says very little and appears not to have reached the stage where he 'joins in play with other children in and outdoors', described by Mary Sheridan (1975).

Recommendations

Joseph will need to be provided with activities which will extend his concentration. For the time being he needs to be guided and limited in his choice. He also needs to be encouraged to join in small group activities.

Pie chart in a differing format

In the previous observation the pie chart showed the time spent on each activity as a percentage of the total time in the diagram, and then the written element described what took place during each segment of time.

It is also possible to record the activities directly onto the chart. This is obviously easier if there are fewer segments.

The following example is for an observation of similar length to the first, but on a child who stayed longer with individual activities.

Observation

Date of observation   20.7.94   **Time commenced**   10.40 a.m.
                                       Time completed   10.57 a.m.

Number of adults   1

Number of children   1

Name of child   Rupert   **Date of birth**   16.6.90
                                Age   4 years 1 month

Aim   To observe a 4-year-old's choice of activity during free play.

Objectives   To observe and record the concentration span and physical development of a 4-year-old.

Setting   In a nursery which has various activities arranged for the children to choose. In one corner there is a climbing frame, which includes a slide. There is a junk modelling table being directed by the teacher, and painting and number games are also available.

Conclusion
Rupert chose to be busy during his 'free choice' period. He began with a quiet activity – looking at a book, and delighted in the pictures for a few minutes. He then became interested in the more physical activity of being on the slide. In the beginning he was cautious in his approach to the climbing frame and slide but as he repeated the activity he gained in confidence and enjoyment. He was then interested in junk modelling, but quickly returned to the slide as the modelling did not really go to plan for him.

Record of observation

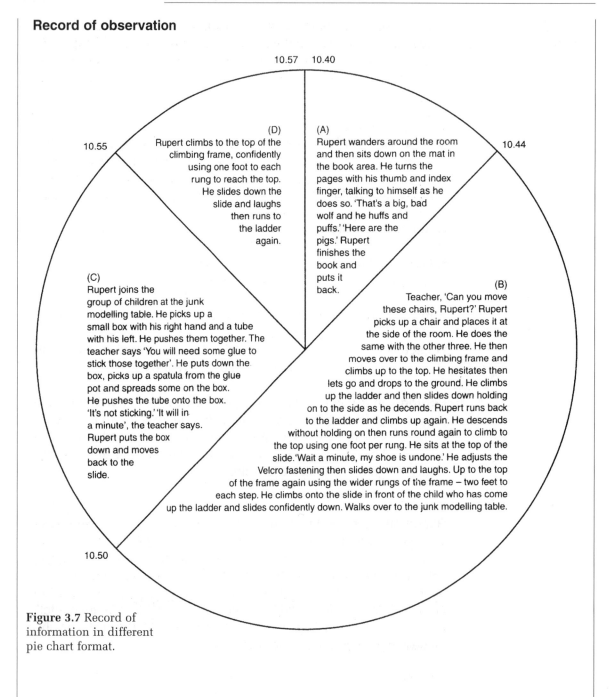

10.57   10.40

(D)
Rupert climbs to the top of the climbing frame, confidently using one foot to each rung to reach the top. He slides down the slide and laughs then runs to the ladder again.

10.55

(A)
Rupert wanders around the room and then sits down on the mat in the book area. He turns the pages with his thumb and index finger, talking to himself as he does so. 'That's a big, bad wolf and he huffs and puffs.' 'Here are the pigs.' Rupert finishes the book and puts it back.

10.44

(C)
Rupert joins the group of children at the junk modelling table. He picks up a small box with his right hand and a tube with his left. He pushes them together. The teacher says 'You will need some glue to stick those together'. He puts down the box, picks up a spatula from the glue pot and spreads some on the box. He pushes the tube onto the box. 'It's not sticking.' 'It will in a minute', the teacher says. Rupert puts the box down and moves back to the slide.

(B)
Teacher, 'Can you move these chairs, Rupert?' Rupert picks up a chair and places it at the side of the room. He does the same with the other three. He then moves over to the climbing frame and climbs up to the top. He hesitates then lets go and drops to the ground. He climbs up the ladder and then slides down holding on to the side as he descends. Rupert runs back to the ladder and climbs up again. He descends without holding on then runs round again to climb to the top using one foot per rung. He sits at the top of the slide. 'Wait a minute, my shoe is undone.' He adjusts the Velcro fastening then slides down and laughs. Up to the top of the frame again using the wider rungs of the frame – two feet to each step. He climbs onto the slide in front of the child who has come up the ladder and slides confidently down. Walks over to the junk modelling table.

10.50

Figure 3.7 Record of information in different pie chart format.

Evaluation

Rupert showed confidence, purpose and persistence in his ability on the climbing frame and slide. He repeated the activity several times, gained in confidence and concentrated on what he was doing. A typical 4-year-old is 'very agile . . . climbs trees and ladders. Climbs stairs and descends confidently one foot to a stair' (see Chapter 7). Four-year-olds enjoy the opportunity for vigorous play in a safe environment and Rupert demonstrated this. He did not concentrate so long on the quieter activities.

Recommendation

Rupert did not concentrate on the junk modelling task because it proved rather difficult. Opportunities to succeed at fine manipulative skills should be introduced and then further observation made. The concentration span of all children can also be increased by an adult taking an interest in what is happening.

Sampling

Time sampling – target child

Using a target child for an observation concentrates on making a detailed record of the behaviour and language of one child. Advantages of using the time sampling method on one child rather than the written/descriptive type of observation are that it helps you to focus on:

Who talked to whom?
Who initiated the social interaction?
Was the target child listening or being encouraged to speak?
How long did the target child spend on an activity – was he/she concentrating or quickly changing from one activity to another?

As stated in Chapter 1, the interval chosen between recording will depend on what your Aims and Objectives are.

Observation

Time sampling – observing a target child

Date of observation   19.3.94   **Time commenced**   8.55 a.m.
                                           Time completed   9.04 a..m.

Number of adults   1

Number of children   2

Names of children   Ryan   **Age**   4 years 7 months
                        Andrew   4 years 9 months

Aim   To observe a target child, Ryan, interacting with a child of similar age while playing with Play-doh.

Objectives To observe and record the social interactions.
To observe and record the language used.

Setting A table in the middle of the 'messy' room. Ryan and Andrew are standing next to each other and both of them have a piece of Play-doh ready. An adult is sitting at one end of the table.

Key TC = Ryan (target child); CI = Andrew (child involved with); A = adult; SP = solitary play; PP = parallel play; Pair P = interactive play.

Record of observation

Time	Activity	Code	Language	Social
8.55	TC puts Play-doh on table and flattens it with his hand. He rolls it back into a ball and then squashes it down a little.	TC	Look – birthday cake.	SP
8.56	TC pushes cake towards CI.	TC–CI	Here! (No response from CI)	PP
8.57	TC takes cake back in front of him and presses it hard. He rolls it into a sausage shape.	TC–CI	Look what I done.	
		CI–TC	What is it?	
		TC–CI	Sausage.	Pair P
8.58	CI stretches over and takes one end of the sausage – it breaks into two pieces.	CI–TC	Two sausages.	Pair P

8.59	TC takes both pieces of Play-doh and rolls them into a ball shape.	CI–TC	Me.
		TC–CI	No. Pair P
9.00	CI reaches over and grabs a round piece of dough. His back is towards TC. TC pushes him in the back.	TC–CI	Mine.
		CI–TC	No.
		TC	Makes a growling noise.
		CI–TC	Share. Here. Pair P
	CI rolls Play-doh to TC.		
9.01	TC and CI roll the dough together into a large ball. They pull it apart and then knead it.		Pair P
9.02	TC reaches across the table and picks up a saucepan. He looks at CI.	TC–CI	Put it in here – it's dinner. Pair P
	TC offers the pan to CI who puts the dough in. They show it to the adult.	TC/CI–A	Look, dinner.
		A–TC/CI	That looks very appetizing. Can I have some please? Pair P

9.03	TC walks round the table and picks up a plate and fork which he takes to A. He puts down the plate and offers the fork.	A–TC	Thank you.	Pair P
9.04	CI moves to one side of A.	CI–A	How many?	
		TC–A	Chips and peas.	Pair P

Conclusion

Before the observation had started both children were involved in playing with the dough, but they were engaged in solitary play. TC had been kneading and flattening the dough and this continued for the first minute of the observation. TC rolled the dough into a cake shape and offered it to CI, who did not respond. On the second offer of the cake CI responded by snatching and pulling the dough. TC retaliated by pushing when he had the opportunity. After a few minutes the incidents were forgotten and the boys played together. They developed the game into imaginative play.

Evaluation

Catherine Lee (1990) says that 'the four year old has a certain amount of control over his emotions, and can communicate both verbally and with body language, often without an adult having to intervene'. All of this type of behaviour is evident in the observation. The boys played well together without adult help although they were quite happy to involve her in their imaginative play.

Recommendations

Provide the dough table with a greater variety of implements so that the imaginative play can be extended and elaborated upon.

Time sampling – group of children

Time sampling also allows you to observe the interactions of a group of children. You can use the written/narrative form but at intervals rather than as a continuous record. This can be useful especially if you have difficulty writing and looking at the same time.   .

Observation

Date of observation   15.7.94   **Time commenced**   10.20 a.m.

Time completed 10.28 a.m.

Number of adults 1

Number of children 5

Names of children	Age
Thomas	3 years 6 months
Christopher	3 years 8 months
Ronan	3 years 1 month
Zara	4 years 2 months
Liam	4 years

Aim   To observe how a group of children use a small-scale train set.

Objectives   To observe and record imaginary play, co-operative play and language used.

Setting   The outdoor play area of a nursery, where several activities have been set up for the children to choose from.

Key to names   T = Thomas; C = Christopher; R = Ronan; Z = Zara; L = Liam; A = adult (nursery nurse).

Record of observation

10.20   Thomas and Christopher have just finished constructing a track for the train. They both have an engine which they are pushing along towards each other.
C–T   'Hang on Thomas.'
T–C   'Wait a minute.'
C–T   'We need a bridge – it's so late.'

10.21   Thomas pushes the train along using both hands. He picks up a truck and joins it to the rest of train.
T–C   'That's my long train.'
C–T   'Shall we pick Gordon up?'

10.22   Ronan joins the group and picks an engine out of the box.
R–T   'Look at me.'

R–C   'Christopher, what is the name of this engine?'
C–T, R   'Let Ronan be Percy or Thomas.'

10.23   Zara and Liam join the group and attempt to take part in the game. Zara leans over to the pieces of track – 'Give me them.'

10.24   The boys are continuing their game and ignoring Zara.
L–T, R 'I need a train.'
C–L, T, R 'I need another bit of track.'

10.25   Zara walks away.
C–L, T, R 'They are coming over the hill. Hello Gordon, can I pass through? Let me past.'

10.26   Christopher is kneeling down pushing the train along. He stops and points at a bridge part.
C–L, T, R 'I need that, I'm going to put it here.'
L–C, T, R 'I've got one passenger.'

10.27   The nursery nurse has joined in and is building a branch line.
A–C, L, R, T 'We can have a small track going out here, can't we?'

10.28   The game is continuing but the tidy-up bell has sounded.

Conclusion

The small group of predominantly boys played co-operatively and involved each one of them. Christopher was more dominant and organizing than the other children and Zara quickly lost interest in the game, once she was unable to have one of the trains. The children have obviously watched some of the series *Thomas the Tank Engine* and used the names for the engines.

Evaluation

The imaginative play was helped by the *Thomas the Tank Engine* series, and the children related well to each other in acting out the story in their group. As Catherine Lee states in *The Growth and Development of Children*, 3- to 4-year-olds: 'enjoy the companionship of other children', 'they talk freely to themselves and to other people', and 'play happily with one or two children or in a small group'. The children talked quite fluently and demonstrated a good vocabulary of words (possibly between 900 and 1,500 words). The group of children centred around one activity and they did take turns, but were not always consistent about this.

Recommendations
Children of this age could possibly be given a longer period of time with an activity in order to develop and extend their imaginary play. They could also then be involved with building more intricate tracks and developing the railway system.

Event sampling

Event sampling is usually linked to observations of children who have a tendency to behave in an anti-social way, such as having temper tantrums or bullying. The aim is to record any incident, what preceded it, and what followed it in order to see if there is any pattern. This will hopefully allow a strategy to be devised to help the child modify their behaviour.

Observation

Date of observation   20.1.94   **Time**   throughout the day.

Number of adults   2

Number of children   Whole class.

Name of child   Ben   **Age**   5 years 4 months

Setting   Reception class.

Aim   To observe Ben's behaviour throughout a day in the class-room.

Objectives   To record any incidents of anti-social behaviour.
To identify what was taking place before the incident.
To record what happened after the incident.

Conclusion
Ben reacted very quickly if someone aggravated him. He tended to take what he wanted without asking. Ben used very little language throughout the day – he was much more likely to use actions. Ben was not always the first to provoke the incident.

Table 3.1 Record of observation.

Date/time	Incident	Previous happening	Who was there	What happened next	Comment
20.1.94 11.20	Ben snatched the rubber from James and James snatched it back.	Writing a story of Ben's choice in work task.	Three other children were present at the table and the teacher was at her desk.	Ben called James a name and hit him on the arm. James shouted and the teacher intervened.	Ben needs to ask politely first; if not, then include the teacher. Ben needs to control his anger.
11.35	Repeat of previous incident.	Continuing to write at the table.	James and Ben were alone at the table. Teacher in book corner.	James called the teacher to intervene and Ben was moved to sit by himself.	Ben reminded again to ask before taking.
1.20	Elliot pushed Ben from behind and Ben fell over.	Children were changing for a PE lesson.	All the children were changing together. Teacher was assisting.	Ben jumped up and pulled Elliot's jumper. Elliot shouted and teacher intervened.	Ben not the initial instigator of this incident.
1.50	Ben screamed because he thought someone had taken his tie.	Children were changing back after PE.	All the children were together.	Several children backed away from Ben looking quite scared. Teacher intervened and found tie.	Ben needs to find an acceptable way to express himself.

Evaluation

Two of the aspects of the social development of a 4-year-old are described in chapter 7 (p. 135) as: 'Likes the companionship of other children and adults but alternates between co-operation and conflict. However, understands the need to use words rather than blows.'

Ben is 5 and still tends to use blows rather than words when he is thwarted or unable to have his own way. However, the other children do seem to have learned this and can provoke Ben to retaliate.

Recommendations

Encourage Ben to express his feelings in acceptable ways, e.g. clay, water, role play.

Listen to both children's explanations after an incident.

Reward good behaviour.

Snapshot

As the name suggests, a snapshot observation samples what is happening at a given moment in time in a specific area. The most usual reason for this type of observation is to discover which areas of the nursery or classroom are being used. It can also provide a method of seeing which children are playing together. The method of recording is quite flexible. You can actually take a photograph or series of photographs and study them at a later date. You can draw a diagram of the setting as you would for a tracking observation and mark in where the children are at a certain time, or you can write a description. The following example is a written description of a nursery class.

Snapshot observation

Date   6.6.94   **Time commenced**   10.15 a.m.
                           Time completed   10.20 a.m.

Number of children   All the children in the nursery.

Ages   2 years 6 months to 4 years.

Number of adults   3

Aim   To observe and record what children are involved in doing within the different areas of the nursery.

Objective   To alter the arrangement of the activities available, or limit the numbers on some activities if necessary.

Setting   The nursery classroom.

Record of observation

The nursery teacher is organizing a finger-painting activity. Sarah, Robert, Philip and Shaheeda are working with her.

The nursery nurse is reading a story to three children – James, Ben and Candy.

Sophie and Jasmin are playing in the sand tray.

Sam, Angela, Helen, Nicola and Neil are in the home corner. Sam and Angela are dressed up as nurses and Nicola has a stethoscope round her neck. Helen and Neil are lying down on the beds.

Julia and Reuben are putting the railway track together and running Thomas the tank engine along it.

Stephanie is wandering from the home corner to the finger-painting activity.

Naomi, Pat and Kelly are being supervised in the water play by the student. They are pouring the water onto a wheel and watching it turn.

Conclusion

All of the children were involved with an activity with the exception of Stephanie, who had just left the home corner for the finger painting. No activity was overcrowded, although the home corner was busy and could not have taken any more children.

Recommendations
There is no need to change the activities at the present time, but the sand and water trays could be moved further apart as the children were a little crowded.

Written/Narrative

The structured and unstructured form of the written narrative were described in Chapter 2. We will now consider the other forms listed at the beginning of this chapter.

Comparative

The comparative observation can be used to evaluate two children of the same age at the same time, and a possible method would be a checklist. For example, you might be assessing the children's ability to carry out tasks or perform physical activities and comparing their results with each other as well as the developmental norms. You could also compare a single child's ability on two different occasions. This is commonly used to monitor any change in behaviour or development when working with special needs children.

The following example illustrates its use to compare a child's ability to indicate a need for the toilet. Children with special needs are regularly monitored, so a baseline is often available if a change is noted. This allows a second observation to be undertaken and an objective evaluation to be made. In the example both the original written/narrative record and the comparative observation are shown.

Original observation

Date   18.1.94   **Time commenced**   10.25 a.m.
                              Time completed   10.31 a.m.

Number of children   1

Number of adults   1

Name of child   Hayley   **Age**   4 years 4 months

Setting   In the toilet area. There are three toilets – the one being used for the observation is lower and has a rail to assist the less able children to be independent.

Aim   To observe a new entrant's ability to use the toilet without assistance.

Objective   To observe and record Hayley's ability to convey a need to use the toilet.

To observe and record Hayley's ability to use the toilet herself.

Record of observation

Hayley is wriggling about and holding herself. She touches the nursery nurse's hand and says something to her. The nursery nurse takes her hand and they walk slowly and rather unsteadily to the toilet together. Once in the toilet area Hayley walks to the adapted cubicle and pushes the door open with her left hand. She walks in, and as she approaches the raised floor she reaches out with her right hand and then places it on the wall before stepping up. Once she has both feet on the raised section she removes her hand and then steps forward before turning around. She stands still and waits. The nursery nurse asks if everything is all right. Hayley smiles and lifts her right hand to point behind the door. The nursery nurse lifts the training seat from behind the door and puts it on the toilet. Hayley has remained quite still, so the nursery nurse encourages her to pull her pants down. Hayley manages to pull down her trousers and pants and the nursery nurse praises her. Hayley lifts up her arms and the nursery nurse lifts her onto the toilet. Hayley smiles and the nursery nurse says she is going to see the child next door but will be back in a minute. While sitting on the toilet Hayley's back is bent and her head is over her knees. When she has finished using the toilet she wriggles off and shuffles to the edge of the raised floor with her pants and trousers around her ankles. At the end of the raised floor, Hayley reaches for the wall with her left hand and steps down. She continues to shuffle forward until she is just outside the toilet door. The nursery nurse returns and asks Hayley if she has finished. Hayley smiles and nods her head. The nursery nurse kneels down and verbally encourages Hayley to pull her pants up. Making no effort to do so, Hayley nods her head and says 'No'. Invited again to try, Hayley moves closer to the wall and unsteadily proceeds to pull up her pants. She tries to pull up the trousers but is unable to do so. The nursery nurse helps, telling her what a good girl she is.

Conclusion

Hayley is aware of when she needs to use the toilet and is able to tell the nursery nurse.

She needs a lot of encouragement, but is able to pull down her trousers and pants.

She is not able to get on the toilet herself, but is able to be left alone for a short period.

Hayley is able to get off the toilet but makes no attempt to dress herself.

If the clothing is loose, e.g. her pants, Hayley is able to pull it up with encouragement, but with tightly fitting clothes like her trousers she needs help.

Evaluation

Hayley is usually able to make her toileting needs known to an adult although she still occasionally has an accident. Due to her physical disability, which affects her motor skills, balance and co-ordination, Hayley often has difficulty removing tight clothing, and needs constant praise and encouragement from an adult. With reference to Catherine Lee (1990), Hayley should be able to use the toilet independently and should have little or no difficulty in removing her clothing. According to Lee's criteria Hayley is performing at the level of a $2\frac{1}{2}$-year-old who 'still has an occasional accident, but is able to ask the adult for the toilet, before she needs to go immediately'.

Hayley attended the nursery on a morning-only basis for the first term. After the Easter holiday she came full time. It was noticed that she was often found wet when toileted at the usual times, and that she no longer asked to use the bathroom. It was decided to carry out an observation over a period of a week to see if Hayley had regressed since attending the nursery on a full-time basis. The observation would consist of a tick chart which the staff would fill in.

Observation

Date   25.4.94   **Time commenced** } The week
                            Time completed } 25–29 April

Number of children   1

Number of adults   5

Name of child   Hayley   **Age**   4 years 7 months.

Setting   The nursery and toilet area.

Aim   To re-assess Hayley's ability to ask for and use the toilet.

Objective   To record the number of times Hayley asks to use the toilet.

To record the number of times Hayley uses the toilet successfully.
To record the number of times Hayley is found to be wet.

Record of observation
The staff were asked to record on the chart if they took Hayley to the toilet:

(a) when asked by Hayley; (b) when they noticed she was wriggling; (c) at the normal toileting times.

They also recorded the number of times Hayley was found to be wet. The tick chart was to be filled in for one week (see p. 63).

Conclusion
Hayley did not ask to use the toilet at all.
The staff noticed Hayley needed the toilet on many occasions.
Hayley used the toilet when taken at the normal times.
Hayley was found to be wet most often after lunch.

Evaluation
Hayley is no longer asking to go to the toilet, which she was able to do three months ago. She appears to have gone backwards in her social training. According to developmental milestones (see Chapter 7, p.131) the $2\frac{1}{2}$-year-old is 'usually dry in the daytime'. Hayley was operating at that level in January.

Recommendations
Discuss the problem with Hayley's mother to see if she is able to make her needs known at home.
If there is also a problem at home ask the doctor to investigate a possible urinary tract infection.
If the problem only occurs at nursery, encourage Hayley to ask for the toilet by rewarding her with a star chart.

Diaries and case studies

Diaries of children's progress can be kept in almost any format. Parents usually keep a record of their children's milestones in the first year which includes dates when they smiled, crawled, walked, etc. and photographs, weight charts and other memorabilia. Parents often compare their child with a friend's child or an older child of their own, but it is not usual to evaluate the progress against developmental norms unless there is undue delay, and therefore cause for concern.

Students are often required to complete a case study on a baby in order to reinforce their knowledge of child development. This usually takes place over a period of six months and the student is able to monitor progress and see the overall change in that time, as well as compare their findings with a recognized developmental milestone checklist.

RECORD OF HAYLEY'S TOILETING for week beginning 25 April

Day.....*Monday*....................

Times (nursery toileting times)

9.00	10.30	11.30	12.30	1.30	2.30

Day.....*Tuesday*....................

Times

9.00	10.30	11.30	12.30	1.30	2.30

Day.....*Wednesday*....................

Times

9.00	10.30	11.30	12.30	1.30	2.30

Day.....*Thursday*....................

Times

9.00	10.30	11.30	12.30	1.30	2.30

Day.....*Friday*....................

Times

9.00	10.30	11.30	12.30	1.30	2.30

Code   ✓ Used the toilet at nursery toilet time.

      ✗ Hayley taken to toilet when staff noticed she was fidgeting.

      ✗ Hayley found to be wet.

      ✗ Hayley asked to go to the toilet.

Figure 3.8 Record of Hayley's toileting.

Case studies in the workplace are usually only carried out when children have some special need. This may be in one area like language, or cover the whole developmental sphere. Case studies always include a description of the child and usually some background information. If students are undertaking a study, therefore, they must have the permission of the guardian or parent of the child. The actual recording method for the observation and the interval between recording will depend on the initial reason for undertaking the study. In the case of students observing a baby, this is normally at monthly intervals in order to see some changes. Sociologists studying groups of children may carry out the observation by interview or questionnaire, and these may continue at yearly intervals or more, over many years. In the case of a child who is receiving training for a speech delay the study may require a review each week and the checklists would be very specific to speech.

The following example is a baby study undertaken over nine months. The reason for monitoring progress was that he was born at 32 weeks' gestation.

Baby study of Mark born 6.8.93

Observation
Baby profile

Mark was born at St Michael's Maternity Hospital 6 August 1993. Mark's mother, Caroline, was 32 weeks pregnant and her expected date of delivery was 1 October. Until the beginning of August Caroline had had a normal pregnancy. She was monitored at the antenatal clinic and as this was her first pregnancy she was booked to be delivered in hospital, with an early discharge if all went well.

On 1 August Caroline woke up with severe pain in her back. She phoned the midwife who visited and arranged for Caroline to be admitted as she was in the early stage of labour. Caroline was put to bed and given drugs to try to stop the labour.

Caroline continued to have some pain and at 10.00 p.m. on 5 August her waters broke. She was moved to the delivery suite and Mark was born at 3.30 a.m. the following morning. He breathed immediately but his weight was only 1.9 kg so he was transferred to the neonatal unit in an incubator.

Caroline made a good recovery and was discharged five days later. She lived fairly close to the hospital so she stayed with Mark during the day, but went home at night. She expressed her breast milk for Mark as he was being tube-fed.

After an initial weight loss Mark started to gain from day 7. He was still being tube-fed as he was unable to suck and he was continuing to be nursed in oxygen in the incubator.

On day 14 Mark stopped breathing. He was resuscitated but it was discovered that his lungs had collapsed. The cause was not known but Mark needed to be put on a ventilator. He was given antibiotics as a precaution.

Mark breathed for himself after five days but he had two more episodes when he had to go back onto the ventilator. Some worries were expressed about the long-term effects of the pressure to his lungs. On 17 September, when Mark was 6 weeks old, he was transferred to a cot and Caroline breast-fed for the first time. Mark tired easily and needed to be tube-fed on occasion but he gained weight and was discharged home on 26 September.

First observation

Date   1.10.93   **Time commenced**   10.30 a.m.
                          Time completed 11.00 a.m.

Name of child   Mark   **Age**   8 weeks

Setting   At home

Aim   To assess Mark's development.

Objective   To record a baseline of Mark's developmental stages for a baby study.

Record of assessment

Mark was lying on his back in his cot. His head was in mid-line with his arms outstretched. When lifted out onto the changing mat Mark's head fell back and needed support. The midwife undressed Mark and weighed him – 3.6 kg. The midwife laid him on his stomach and he moved his head round to look at his mother.

Mark started to cry and his mother turned him over and talked to him as she put his clothes back on. Mark quietened and concentrated on his mother's face. Caroline tried an experiment by poking her tongue out and after a moment Mark copied her.

Caroline prepared herself to feed Mark. When he was offered the breast he turned his head and latched onto the nipple quickly. He sucked well for five minutes. He made occasional grunts as he fed and his toes curled in satisfaction. At the end of the feed Mark concentrated on Caroline's face and he smiled when spoken to.

Conclusion
Mark weighed 3.6 kg.
Mark responded to his mother by copying her gestures and smiling. When laid on his stomach he lifted and turned his head. When he was lifted up his head fell back.

Evaluation
According to the developmental milestones in Chapter 7 Mark's weight is average for a new-born baby. Although he is 8 weeks old his expected birth date was this week. His head lag when lifted out of the cot is also more like that of a new-born than a baby of 8 weeks. However, he is smiling and responding to his mother.

Mark is gestationally a new-born baby but chronologically he is 8 weeks old. His development according to the normal milestones is somewhere in between the two.

Second observation

Date 7.2.94   **Age** 6 months.   **Time commenced** 2.15 p.m.
                                            Time completed   2.50 p.m.

Record of observation
Mark was lying on his stomach on the changing mat. He lifted himself up onto his forearms and looked around the room when he heard the noise of his food being mixed in the kitchen. Caroline came into the room and Mark gurgled as she lifted him into the baby relax chair. He sat up quite straight with support. He ate his mashed vegetables before enjoying a breast feed.

At the end of the feed Caroline stood him up on her lap. Mark took his weight on his legs and bounced up and down before snuggling into Caroline's chest. After a few minutes he started to wriggle and Caroline put him down on his stomach on the changing mat again. He pushed up onto his forearms and looked around then started crying. Caroline turned him over and gave him a rattle. He held it for a few seconds before letting it go. He started to cry again so Caroline changed him and put him down for a sleep. He continued to grizzle for a while and then fell asleep.

Conclusion
Mark is able to lift himself up onto his forearms to look around when he is on his stomach.
He is able to sit with support and to support his own weight when held standing.
Mark is not able to roll over or to hold a rattle for long.

He recognizes familiar sounds like lunch being prepared.

Evaluation

According to the milestones in Chapter 7 a 6-month-old baby is able to support his own weight when held standing, is able to sit with support and will recognize familiar sounds and react to them. Mark is doing all these things. A 6-month-old can usually push up onto their hands and roll over, and hold a rattle and transfer it to the other hand. Mark is not able to do these yet.

Third observation

Date 5.5.94   **Age** 9 months.   **Time commenced** 12.30 p.m.
                                      Time completed 12.50 p.m.

Record of observation

Mark had just woken from his morning sleep. He was sitting up in the cot calling out. When Caroline entered the room he stopped shouting and lifted up his arms to be taken out.

Caroline laid him on the changing mat and took off the wet nappy. Mark wriggled and turned over. Caroline turned him back and gave him a toy duck to hold. Mark looked at it then put it in his mouth. Caroline carried him downstairs and sat him on the floor in front of the television. Mark sat quite well but then he reached out for a toy brick and fell over. He cried to be sat up again.

Caroline sat him in the high chair and gave him a piece of toast. Mark picked it up and began to suck it.

Conclusion

Mark is able to sit himself up and call for attention.

He can roll over and sits quite well unsupported but he falls over when he reaches out for a toy.

He can hold a toy and transfer it from hand to hand and he finger-feeds.

Evaluation

According to developmental milestones the 9-month-old can shout for attention, examine things with the mouth and finger-feed well. Mark is able to do these.

The 9-month-old is also able to sit for long periods and lean forward to reach a toy without overbalancing. Mark is able to sit well but still overbalances when trying to reach a toy.

The 9-month-old can often pull to stand and start to crawl but Mark has not done this yet. He is still a little behind in his milestones according to his chronological age.

Fourth observation

Date 6.8.94   **Age** First birthday.   **Time commenced** 2.30 p.m.
                                                Time completed 3.00 p.m.

Record of observation

Mark was sitting on the floor playing with a wrapped parcel. He was trying to pull the paper off and put it in his mouth. His mum called to him and he turned round to look at her then crawled over and pulled himself up using her skirt to assist him. He edged sideways along the settee and grabbed hold of a ball. When it fell off the settee he let go and dropped to the floor to crawl after it.

There was a knock at the door and Mark turned round to see who would come in. When his dad came in he squealed with delight and lifted his arms to be picked up. He bounced up and down in dad's arms and shouted 'da-da-da'.

Caroline moved towards the door and called to Mark. He stopped and turned to look at her.

'Do you want a drink?' she asked.

'Dink', he said.

Caroline went out and returned with a drink of juice in a feeding cup. Mark took it in both hands and drank it down.

Conclusion

Mark is able to crawl well and pull himself up to stand.
When something falls he watches where it goes and crawls after it.
He vocalizes and tries to copy speech.
He responds to his own name.
He is able to feed himself using a feeding cup.

Evaluation

According to the milestones in Chapter 7 the 1-year-old is crawling, pulling to stand and walking round the furniture. They drop toys and watch them fall then look in the right direction when they roll out of sight. They babble and may say two or three single words. They are able to drink from a cup with a little assistance. Mark is able to do all of these.

Overall evaluation

Mark was born 8 weeks early and had severe breathing problems. He had some developmental delay up to the age of 9 months but he had caught up completely by a year.

Checklists

The example given in Chapter 1 showed a checklist for recording a group of children's physical abilities. The two following examples show how checklists can be used for individual children. The first compares a child's behaviours with those set out in a recognized developmental scale and requires you to prepare a list of those norms to be completed over a period of time. The second example looks at one area, concentration, over a fairly short period of time. It requires you to think carefully about what you want to find out and how to set about it. In this example it was decided that recording the amount of time the child was *on task/off task* would give a good guide as to whether she was interested, and therefore concentrating.

Observation

Checklist using norms of social development according to a recognized scale

Date of observation   10.6.94 to 15.6.94

Number of adults   1   **Time commenced**
                           Time completed   } Over a few days.

Number of children   1

Name of child   Elizabeth   **Age**   4 years 7 months.

Aim   To see if a $4\frac{1}{2}$-year-old child meets the 'norms' for her developmental progress.

Objective   To observe and record the developmental achievement of a $4\frac{1}{2}$-year-old, according to the norms set out by Mary Sheridan (1995).

Setting   In a nursery, over a period of days, with normal activities being undertaken.

The 'norm' according to *Children's Development and Progress*	Yes	No	Comments
1. Affectionate and confiding	✓		Elizabeth holds her friend's hand and whispers to her as they sit together.

Table 3.2 Checklist of social development.

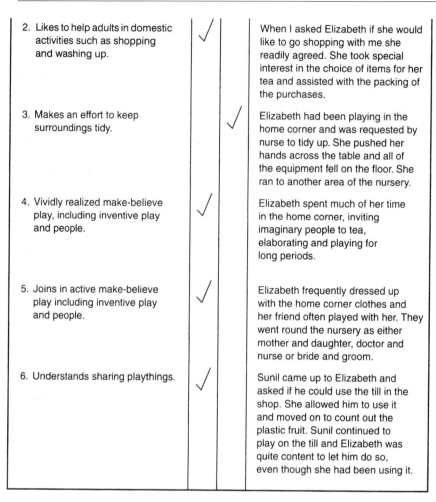

2. Likes to help adults in domestic activities such as shopping and washing up.	✓	When I asked Elizabeth if she would like to go shopping with me she readily agreed. She took special interest in the choice of items for her tea and assisted with the packing of the purchases.
3. Makes an effort to keep surroundings tidy.	✓	Elizabeth had been playing in the home corner and was requested by nurse to tidy up. She pushed her hands across the table and all of the equipment fell on the floor. She ran to another area of the nursery.
4. Vividly realized make-believe play, including inventive play and people.	✓	Elizabeth spent much of her time in the home corner, inviting imaginary people to tea, elaborating and playing for long periods.
5. Joins in active make-believe play including inventive play and people.	✓	Elizabeth frequently dressed up with the home corner clothes and her friend often played with her. They went round the nursery as either mother and daughter, doctor and nurse or bride and groom.
6. Understands sharing playthings.	✓	Sunil came up to Elizabeth and asked if he could use the till in the shop. She allowed him to use it and moved on to count out the plastic fruit. Sunil continued to play on the till and Elizabeth was quite content to let him do so, even though she had been using it.

Table 3.2 (cont'd)

Conclusion
Elizabeth was observed over a period of several days and the norms were used as statements about a $4\frac{1}{2}$-year-old's expected development. Several opportunities arose to observe the behaviours apart from the ones recorded.

Evaluation
Elizabeth was typical in most of her social developmental milestones. She did not, however, attempt to tidy up on any occasion, and this was untypical behaviour according to the checklist and compared with the other children in the nursery.

Recommendations
Elizabeth is encouraged to tidy up after her play, whatever type of activity she has undertaken. Other areas of development are to be observed in a similar way.

Observation

Checklist – pre-coded for time and concentration on task

Date of observation   18.5.94

Number of adults   1   **Time commenced**   12.50 p.m.

Number of children   4   **Time completed**   1.05 p.m.

Name of child   Karla   **Age**   4 years 6 months.

Aim   To observe a group of children, and in particular one child, to record how long she spent on task and engrossed in what she was doing.

Objective   To see how a $4\frac{1}{2}$-year-old concentrates on what she is doing, and how co-operatively the children play without any adult intervention.

Setting   A table-top game of Racing Snails being played with board and dice by four children in a nursery.

Time	On task – engrossed	On task – not engrossed	Off task – quiet	Off task – disruptive
12.50	✓			
12.51			✓	
12.52			✓	
12.53	✓			
12.54			✓	
12.55	✓			
12.56			✓	
12.57	✓			
12.58			✓	
12.59	✓			
1.00			✓	
1.01	✓			
1.02	✓			
1.03			✓	
1.04	✓			

Table 3.3 Record of observation.

Conclusion

The game lasted for 15 minutes and there was a lot of co-operation by all of the participants. There was good evidence of socialization and use of language (although this is not evident from the recording of the observation). Children took turns with the dice and moved the snails in the proper way for most of the time.

Evaluation

Karla concentrated for the majority of the time that the game was being played. She co-operated well with the group of children, which is typical for a 4-year-old (see Chapter 7). She was able to take turns and to approach the game in a reasonable manner. Her concentration span as good compared with some of the other children.

Recommendations

Karla's concentration span was good, so more pre-reading and pre-writing activities could be encouraged so as to maintain this level of concentration, and prepare her for school next term.

The method used was suitable to record concentration span and enabled the recorder to demonstrate this. However, it would be possible to undertake an observation of the same activity to find out different aspects of the child's development. As noted in the conclusion, a lot of language took place which was not obvious in the chart. There was an occasional dispute about the number of moves to be made or the number thrown on the dice. This did not essentially interrupt the game but would identify another aspect of the children's developmental stage. It is important therefore to consider the method and aims carefully before undertaking an observation.

Observations Using Other Media for Recording

Figure 3.2 (p. 36) showed various media for recording your observations. We have demonstrated the use of graphs (block), diagrams (tracking) and written material. It is not possible to show you the use of tape and video but do try if you have the opportunity. They enable you to record longer periods in detail and you can repeatedly play them back in order to make your evaluations. Tape is obviously very useful for looking at language and children's understanding of why things happen, e.g. using it to record their ideas about where rain comes from. You might need to practise to enable the children to get used to working with tape. Do remember that the recorder will pick up all the surrounding noise, so choose somewhere quiet.

The last observation uses a photograph and a copy of the child's work to record the results. It would require the permission of the parent if you intended to use it as part of your portfolio, as the photo would mean the child is identifiable. Using the children's work as evidence is very useful for some types of observation, especially those assessing intellectual/cognitive skills.

Observation

Date   6.7.94   **Time commenced**   2.15 p.m.
                           Time completed   2.35 p.m.

Name of child   Samantha   **Age**   6 years 2 months.

Setting   The construction area of a year 1 classroom during a free-play session.

Aim   To discover a 6-year-old's ability to draw what they see.

Objective   To observe and record a child's ability to draw a representation of a construction she built using wooden bricks.

Record of observation
Samantha had been carefully constructing a building using a selection of wooden bricks of various shapes. She worked alongside a group of other children but did not communicate with them as she was concentrating very hard. When she completed the task I asked her if it would be possible to draw a picture of the castle so that we could keep a record. She referred to the structure frequently as she drew and seemed quite pleased with the result.

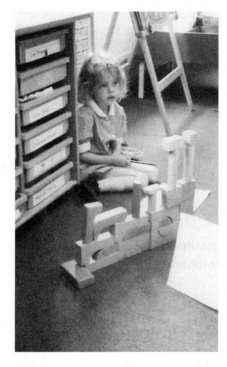

Figure 3.9 Samantha and her drawing.

Conclusion

As the photograph and drawing show, Samantha was able to make a very good attempt at recording the building in some detail. She noticed where the different shapes were in relation to each other and had the sizes quite well in proportion.

Evaluation

Samantha demonstrated that she could 'draw more realistic and complicated pictures', one of the developmental milestones for a 6-year-old (see Chapter 7, p. 137). According to the teacher she was ahead of many of the children in the class who were of similar age, or even older.

You have now had the opportunity to read examples of the various types of observation you can use to record and evaluate children's behaviour.

There now follow some suggestions for Aims and Objectives that you might like to use to practise the skill for yourself. First decide which method you think will give you the best result. There are no 'right' answers; you should try them out and see. If you find one method unsuitable then try another.

Suggestions for Aims and Objectives

1. AIM: To observe the physical ability of a 7-month-old baby.
    OBJECTIVE: To watch movement from the supine to prone position, and to observe the head, shoulder and neck movements.
2. AIM: To observe the balance and the movement of a 9-month-old baby.
    OBJECTIVE: To watch how a 9-month-old can reach the sitting position without help and how he/she can sit without support for a considerable time.
3. AIM: To observe the hand-to-eye co-ordination and fine motor skills of a 2-year-old.
    OBJECTIVE: To look at the ability of a 2-year-old to guide hand movements with his/her eyes, and to see if a preferred hand is used.
4. AIM: To observe a new entrant to the nursery.
    OBJECTIVE: To watch how the child integrates and socializes with the other children, and to identify what helps a child settle into a new group.
5. AIM: To observe a 4-year-old's language development.
    OBJECTIVE: To observe the vocabulary, the conversational ability and the questioning that a 4-year-old child is using.
6. AIM: To observe a 5-year-old child's social development.
    OBJECTIVE: To observe a 5-year-old's ability to relate to adults and to integrate within a small and large group of children.
7. AIM: To observe why children are attracted to an activity in the nursery setting.
    OBJECTIVE: To see what initially attracts the child, what keeps him/her at the activity and whether the activity has a satisfactory outcome.
8. AIM: To observe a 4-year-old during a free-choice session.
    OBJECTIVE: To note the choice of activities, and to observe the length of concentration on each activity.

9.   AIM: To observe a group of 4-year-olds in the home corner.
     OBJECTIVE: To see if children interact and engage in elaborate and prolonged imaginative play.

10. AIM: To observe a small group of 5-year-olds playing with clay.
     OBJECTIVE: To observe and record the manipulative skills and the imagination of 5-year-olds while playing with this tactile material.

11. AIM: To observe a 5-year-old during an outdoor play session.
     OBJECTIVE: To observe and record whether he/she is able to run, skip, climb, jump, throw and catch a ball, and is agile and energetic.

12. AIM: To observe a 3-year-old painting.
     OBJECTIVE: To see and record how the child experiments with the paint and brush.

13. AIM: To observe the interaction between two boys of similar age (7) while playing with a construction set.
     OBJECTIVE: To see how the boys co-operate in the task and record the language they use.

14. AIM: To observe the gross motor skills of a class of 4-year-olds.
     OBJECTIVE: To record their ability to balance, climb and control a ball.

15. AIM: To observe the social skills of a 3-month-old baby.
     OBJECTIVE: To identify how a young baby communicates before language emerges, and how she/he shows pleasure by facial expressions.

16. AIM: To observe the motor skills of a 1-year-old.
     OBJECTIVE: To identify how mobile a 1-year-old is, and which method is used most often when moving about during the day.

17. AIM: To identify how a 6-month-old baby spends a day.
     OBJECTIVE: To record what proportions of the day are spent awake, asleep, crying, feeding, playing, etc.

18. AIM: To observe a group of 5-year-olds while participating in a science experiment.
     OBJECTIVE: To watch a group of children observing, analysing, concluding and predicting the results of a series of experiments.

4

Extending and Utilizing Your Observations

At the end of this chapter you will be able to:

Observe and record in increased detail.
Understand why your observations are important to the children in your care.
Recognize the need to work with others to achieve your aims.
Understand the roles and responsibilities of professionals working with children.

By the end of the previous chapter you should have been able to satisfy yourself that the observations you have completed conform to three main criteria:

1. You have observed children carefully enough and for sufficient time to see what they are capable of. This may mean observing on more than one occasion or using different methods.
2. You have read widely and understand why children behave in the ways that they do. You know the normal developmental stages.
3. You have used your knowledge to plan activities and routines which will encourage children to move forward. These are challenging enough to enable the children to feel a sense of achievement, but are not beyond the children's ability.

Once you are well practised in observation you will find that you tend to assess children throughout your working day. These assessments help with planning, but we can still make assumptions about a child because we only notice them at certain times. If we do not take the time to make detailed observations we may miss important facts.

As Joan Tough (1976) found when talking to teachers about their class, one commented 'I haven't any quiet ones, I wish I had, all my children talk all the time.'

Amongst those children on whom she ran a sampling check was Sheila, and these were the teacher's comments after observation:

> Sheila's not very big for her age and I think I must have overlooked her before. She gave an answer when I spoke to her, just a short one, but I couldn't tell what she said. I never saw her speak to anyone else and much of the time she was on her own, playing with jigsaws or pegboard. In fact, she never moved from the table until playtime. I think she needs help trying out other things and in approaching other children and I must find out what her speech difficulties are. (p. 47)

This observation was undertaken in a reception class. The teacher understood that Sheila's behaviour was not what is expected for the age group.

How do you know what to expect a child will be able to do?

You will learn from working with children as well as from research and development charts. You need to know what to expect so that you can advise parents or refer the child for more specialist assessment. Take speech for example. A child of 30 months has joined your nursery and his only words are 'mum', 'dad', 'ball'. The parents want to know if this small vocabulary is normal for this age.

You cannot answer if you have no idea of normal speech development. As Harold Fishbein (1984, p. 7) noted:

> As soon as we can describe a developmental sequence and locate a child on that sequence we can begin to make some reasonable judgements about his rate of development, whether behind or ahead of other children, and to make some predictions as to what to expect next.

Language is important as it is often linked to ability.

> Until the child can express his ideas, intentions and needs through the use of language, other people can only guess what it is he wants them to know from his gestures and actions, from the tone of his voice and from his facial expression. (Tough, 1976, p. 8)

Language relates not only to the number of words a child can use but also to how much a child understands of what is being said. We cannot gain a true picture of a child's ability unless she has the opportunity to demonstrate what she is capable of. We need to be aware of the cultural, social, emotional and physical factors which may affect our evaluation.

Indeed, Margaret Donaldson believes that 'failure is a perverse inability of the teacher and student to come to terms with the communication problem' (Bruner, in Foreword of Grieve and Hughes, 1990).

This is not usually a conscious decision, but as children grow older we begin to rely heavily on an understanding of language, both spoken and written, in order to evaluate progress. Many people who did not have their dyslexia recognized have testified to the trauma this caused in their lives. In a discussion of writing, Miranda Jones (1990, in Grieve and Hughes, 1990) comments:

> The importance which society places on literacy and logic means that children who find it difficult to learn are quickly made to feel inadequate. The teacher's task, therefore, is to build on what the child has already discovered about reading and writing. Obviously this will be facilitated by knowing what sort of a knowledge base is already in existence.

This is why a thorough assessment using developmental checklists (see Chapter 7) and detailed observation is so important. Observations should become 'records of achievement' with recommendations for targets for further achievement.

Consider the following situation:

Mrs Wallace brings her daughter Sophie (3 years and 4 months) to your nursery for a visit. The family has recently moved into the area after living abroad for 2 years. She has not attended a nursery before and her mother is quite anxious about how she will settle. She stays for about an hour with her mother and does not attempt to move away from her. When approached by staff she hides her head. A further visit is arranged and this follows a similar pattern. After discussion between the manager and Mrs Wallace it is decided that Sophie will come to the nursery on three mornings a week. When asked if Sophie has any special name for the toilet, drink, etc. so staff will know what she wants, Mrs Wallace replies 'no'.

Sophie is brought to the nursery by her father, who says that his wife can't face having to leave her and see her possibly upset. You help Sophie to take her coat off and stay with her for the morning. After talking to the manager Mr Wallace says goodbye and leaves. Sophie looks at her dad leaving and begins to cry quietly. You take her over to a table where a group of children are doing puzzles and let her sit on your lap while you start to do a puzzle. You ask Sophie if she would like to help but she does not respond. After a few minutes she stops crying but still shows no sign of wanting to join in. You take her round the nursery to look at the various areas to see if she appears to be interested in anything but she clings to you. Most of the children want to play outside before snack time so you put Sophie's coat on and show her the bikes, cars and prams. She takes hold of a pram but another child comes rushing by on a bike, so she grips your hand again and stays by your side for the rest of the session. At snack time Sophie is offered milk and juice; she points to the juice. After snack time the children sit on the mat to listen to a story. Sophie sits quietly and appears to be listening but she does not respond to any of the questions. At the end of the morning, when her mother comes to collect her, she smiles and runs over to her.

A pattern develops over the next few sessions. Sophie cries initially but this doesn't last long. She stays fairly close to you and will sit drawing or completing a jigsaw. She responds to questioning with nods or pointing. She watches other children playing but does not attempt to join in. She seems to dislike loud noise. If she needs something, such as going to the toilet, she pulls you towards the door.

At first you attribute this behaviour to the fact that Sophie is shy. She is an only child who has not been used to mixing and being separated from her mother, but as time goes by you begin to wonder if something is wrong.

What should you do?

First, raise your concerns at the staff meeting: have others noticed the same pattern of behaviour? Your manager will then probably suggest that you carry out an observation before she discusses Sophie with her parents.

What are your main concerns?

You may decide that you are interested in finding out whether Sophie makes any attempt to talk to staff or children during her time at the nursery. You may want to see if she tries to join in any activity involving other children.

> *How are you going to find this out, remembering that you want to give Sophie the best possible chance to give a true picture of her ability?*

Activity

Look at page 49. If you agree that time sampling is a possible solution, write out your aim and objectives. Then decide how often you need to observe and over what time period.

If your observation or observations confirm that Sophie does not attempt to play with other children and does not talk to anyone in the nursery, then you need to consider whether this is what you expect of a child of her age.

How are you going to do that?

You can compare her behaviour with that of other children of the same age in the nursery. You also need to read about the social and language skills of 3½-year-old children. The fact that you noticed her behaviour suggests that she was not behaving like the other children of similar age. Developmental charts show that a 3-year-old has 'Extensive vocabulary which is usually intelligible even to strangers,' and 'Begins to join in games with other children and to share, but still needs to be in small groups.' (See Chapter 7 on developmental milestones.)

You need to understand how speech and social skills develop in order to suggestion further investigation and action planning.

Remember, Plan and Carry Out Activity + Observation + Evaluation
= Action

Joan Tough, in *Listening to Children Talking* (1976), has a chapter on 'The child who does not talk'. Although the research was carried out over twenty years ago, many of her findings are relevant today. Three main reasons for lack of speech are generally accepted: physical abnormality, lack of stimulation, emotional problems. Joan Tough used extensive observation as an assessment tool but also commented that it is vital to talk to the family to gain a fuller picture. In this instance it would be very important to arrange an interview with Mr and Mrs Wallace to see if Sophie talks at home and to find out what opportunities she has had for playing with other children. This meeting would probably be set up by your manager, but you might be asked to attend as you are the person who has had the most contact with Sophie.

At the interview Mr Wallace admits that he has not spent a great deal of time with Sophie. His job involves long hours and she is often in bed when he comes home. Mrs Wallace is a very quiet person herself and when she lived abroad had not felt very confident about going out when she did not speak the language well. She and Sophie spent a lot of time together drawing, cooking and playing games but she realizes that they did not do much singing or talking about what was going on as this seemed rather a strange thing to do on your own with a child. Sophie had not been to the local kindergarten as there were no other English-speaking children in the area. Both parents were reasonably happy with Sophie's behaviour. She had walked at a year, was toilet trained by 18 months and she seemed to understand when asked to do something. They admitted that she only used a very occasional word, relying on the fact that they understood her gestures.

How would you expect your manager to proceed?

It appears that Sophie is a much-loved child but that she may not have been spoken to very much. She has not had the opportunity to mix with other children. Her physical and cognitive development are within normal limits. Her drawing suggests that she is even a little ahead.

One possibility which should occur to you is that Sophie may have some degree of hearing loss. The family has been living abroad so she may not have been monitored by the Health Visitor on a regular basis. Mrs Wallace says that a doctor was available for staff and their families. Sophie had her immunizations but she had not had any screening tests. The family has just registered with the GP so it was suggested that an appointment with the Health Visitor would be a good idea. If it was found that Sophie had hearing loss and no specific reason such as an infection was detected, the Health Visitor would probably refer her for a more exact test with the audiologist. It would also be a good idea to make a referral to the speech therapist as these appointments often take quite a long time to come through. (See pp. 90–3 for descriptions of professional roles.)

A hearing loss is often the reason why a child fails to talk, but if you have read widely you will also realize that 'Pre-school language impairment, or the late acquisition of speech, are important and useful early indicators of dyslexia' (Ott, 1997).

There are several other indicators and the speech therapist or educational psychologist will take a careful history before making a diagnosis. It will not be up to you or your manager to make these decisions but as you can see it was your observation which led to the matter being investigated. Hopefully there will not be a long term problem, but the longer it is left the more likely the problem will intensify. In the meantime you should be planning activities to encourage sounds and speech, and making sure that you:

- Look at Sophie when you talk.
- Use gestures to re-inforce your instructions.
- Name objects as you play with them.
- Encourage interaction in small groups without too much distraction.
- Praise and encourage any attempts to interact with other children or make sounds.

You then need to continue to observe and record her achievements. This becomes a planning cycle.

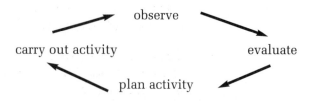

This cycle is important for all children, but especially so for those with a special need. Observation is the only way to know if a plan of action is successful or if changes are necessary.

The next two observations demonstrate how two children (Colin and Ryan) with apparently similar problems – an inability to act in ways socially and emotionally appropriate for their age – actually have very different problems and require different action plans.

Colin (3 years, 10 months) used to enjoy coming to nursery but lately has become very tearful and angry when his mother leaves. He refuses to join in games and throws himself to the floor when asked to join in the singing or go outside on the big toys. His spoken language is excellent, his drawing detailed and he can recognize several words. It is decided to observe Colin by time sampling over a period of an hour each morning for four mornings to see if anything is triggering the behaviour.

Observation

Day 1

09.00 Colin is brought to nursery by his mother. He tugs her back towards the door shouting 'No, no.' Mother tries to reason with him and asks him to take his coat off. He pulls it more closely round him and continues to scream. Mother is becoming more agitated so a nursery nurse takes hold of him, and suggests mother say goodbye and leave. Colin kicks the nursery nurse as she tries to restrain him from running out of the door after her.

09.10 The children are sitting on the mat for registration. Colin is sitting with the nursery nurse looking at a book. He points to words, asking 'What does that say?' When asked to be quiet to listen for his name, he throws the book, hitting one of the other children. The nursery nurse asks him to say sorry but he looks away and refuses.

09.20 The children have been asked to choose what they plan to do this morning. Colin is sitting in the writing area. He is absorbed in the activity, and when asked what he is doing he looks quite indignant before answering 'I'm writing a letter to my grandma.'

09.30 Colin is still in the writing area. He is reading the letter back to himself. He appears satisfied with his work. He asks for an envelope to put it in.

09.40   Colin has moved into the book corner. He has arranged several of the soft toys in a row, and is reading a story to them. His voice goes up and down as he assumes the different characters in Goldilocks and the Three Bears.

09.50   Colin is still in the book corner. The children have been asked to start clearing away but Colin makes no attempt to put his book down. Another child comes over and starts to put the toys back on the shelf. Colin looks up and sees what is happening. He shouts 'No, don't do that, they are listening to a story.' When the child says it is clearing-up time, he grabs the teddybear she is holding and attempts to take it back. When she holds on he bends over to bite. (Observation suspended as you intervene.)

Day 2

09.00   Colin is brought to nursery by his grandmother. He is sullen when left, but does not scream. He takes his coat off and sits hunched up in the book corner. When approached by other children he puts his foot out to try and trip them. They move away and sit on the mat.

09.10   At registration Colin is still sitting in the corner. A nursery nurse sits beside him and tries to encourage him to move closer to the group. He ignores her. When asked what he plans to do this morning, he chooses the writing area.

09.20   Colin is sitting in the writing area looking into space. When asked what he wants to do, he says he is thinking up a story to write. He has folded some pieces of paper up to resemble a book.

09.30   Colin is engrossed in writing his story. Two other children have moved into the area but he ignores them. A child leans across the table to put a colouring pencil back into the pot. He accidentally makes a mark on Colin's page, which sends him into a rage. He stamps, shouts 'You've ruined it', and proceeds to tear the book up. The other child looks startled and begins to cry. A nursery nurse assures him it was an accident. She suggests Colin might like to try something else. He stamps out of the area and goes over to the home corner. He throws the bedding from the cot onto the floor and then sits under the table.

09.40   Colin is still under the table. He refuses to pick up the bedding.

09.50   Colin is still under the table. Attempts to coax him out have all failed. It is now tidy-up time and the other children tidy up around him. (It is decided to ignore Colin while continuing to observe.)

10.00   Colin has moved out from under the table. He has taken out a jigsaw puzzle and put it on the table. The other children are sitting on the floor holding what they have made, painted etc., ready to tell the rest of the group what they have been doing. The nursery nurse asks Colin to come and sit down. He ignores her so one of the staff takes him by the hand and sits with him. When he is asked what he has done this morning, he says he wrote a story 'but it got ruined'.

Day 3

You are beginning to realize that Colin's behaviour seems to be linked to interruptions when he is absorbed in an activity. He also appears to stay on his own for most of the time.

To find out if this is the case you decide to observe for the whole morning.

To make recording easier you monitor Colin at fifteen minute intervals using the following headings.

Time	Activity	Interactions
09.15	Colin arrives late with mother. She explains he had a temper tantrum.	Refuses to speak to anyone.
09.30	Doing some colouring, being very careful not to go over the lines.	Chatting to nursery nurse about a visit to the zoo.
09.45	'Writing' about the zoo visit.	None.
10.00	Sitting on the mat with other children, telling the nursery nurse about his story	Gives a very full explanation of what he had been writing.
10.15	Having juice and a biscuit at the table.	None.
10.30	The children have gone outside to play. Colin is beside the wall. He is scowling and occasionally kicks the wall.	Muttering under his breath.

10.45	Takes off coat and hangs it up. Hurries over to the table and sits down with his group. Looks at the picture of the three Billy Goats on his worksheet. When the nursery nurse (N.N.) asks if anyone knows which is the smallest he puts up his hand and is picked to answer. 'This is the smallest, this is the middle-sized and this is the biggest. He isn't frightened by the Troll.'	Smiles at nursery nurse.
11.00	Colin is drawing his version of the story.	Talking to N.N.
11.15	The children are singing nursery rhymes. Colin is being calmed down after an outburst.	Shouting 'I want to go.'
11.30	Sitting listening to a story tape.	None.
11.45	Wandering around the nursery while the others are collecting their work to take home.	
12.00	Collected by mother.	Chats away about the story when asked what he did.

Colin's mother is aware that he has been observed and is anxious to discuss his problem. He does not have similar outbursts at home. He has two older sisters and appears to relate well to them. A meeting is arranged for the following morning.

Day 4

Colin arrives at the nursery in a rage. He is shouting 'I told you I didn't want to come. I don't want to play. I want to work.'

He and his mother are invited into the office and the manager waits for Colin to calm down. She then asks him if he can explain why he doesn't like coming to nursery. He replies that he doesn't like playing, he wants to do work. When asked 'what work', he replies 'reading and writing and the computer'. The manager asks if he would like to do some work now and he agrees. This allows the discussion to go on without Colin. Mrs Edwards is asked about the sort of things Colin does at home. It becomes apparent that he is very involved with language activities and has a lot of 'educational' toys. His father spends time helping him play word and number-matching games on the computer and his older sisters also encourage him.

Evaluation

When this information is added to the behaviour observed at the nursery it becomes very clear that Colin is frustrated if he is unable to complete a task. It also confirms that he is not very good at socializing with his peer group. His cognitive development is well advanced, but he is likely to experience difficulty at school if his social and emotional problems are not addressed.

With this knowledge it is now possible to plan with his mother. Perhaps he could have a friend to tea or to go on an outing with the family. In the nursery Colin will still be encouraged to do the activities he enjoys, but he will be warned when only 5 minutes are left so that he can plan to finish. At the computer he might be able to help another child.

Children who are naturally shy or prefer to work on their own will not change dramatically, but they can learn how to co-operate with others, and to experience some of the pleasures of shared activities.

The second observation is of Ryan who has just had his fourth birthday. Ryan has poor speech. It is difficult to understand what he says and he does not use sentences. He can be very disruptive and often finds himself in trouble. It is decided to shadow him for a whole morning. This takes up all the time for one member of staff, but it is hoped to discover more about why Ryan has problems with the rest of the group.

Observation

09.00 Ryan bursts into the nursery and runs through to the coat area. He pulls off his coat and throws it onto the peg. It misses and falls on the floor. A nursery nurse asks him to pick it up, but he has gone. He goes into the main nursery and selects a plastic giraffe from the shelf which he plays with, making it walk along the table.

09.10 The nursery nurse is sitting in the book area with the rest of the children. 'Come and sit down for registration, Ryan.' Ryan continues to play with the giraffe, so she stands up and reaches over to take his hand. Ryan struggles and pulls away. He hides under a table and begins to 'eat' the giraffe. (He is ignored for a while but then another member of staff takes the giraffe away and sits him on her lap. He remains seated sucking his thumb.) The group are deciding where they would like to work first this morning. 'Where are you going to choose, Ryan?' Without removing his thumb, he mumbles something. 'Take your thumb away, I can't hear you.' The nursery nurse removes his thumb and Ryan says 'blocks'.

09.20   Ryan has built a ramp and walkway with the large wooden blocks. He has been assisted by another child. There has been no conversation but they appear to have agreed where things should go. Another child comes over and picks up one of the blocks from the walkway. Ryan looks up and runs over shouting 'No, no'. He pushes the child who hastily drops the block. A member of staff tells Ryan not to push as it isn't kind. Ryan proceeds to pile up the blocks and sit on them. Anyone who comes near is scowled at. One of the other children has told a member of staff that Ryan won't let her play. The nursery nurse goes over and asks Ryan to share but he shakes his head. She tries to reason with him and when this doesn't work she moves him off the blocks. He races round the room bumping into several children.

09.35   The children are putting on coats to go outside. Ryan is persuaded to fasten his jacket and runs out to claim one of the bikes. He pedals well and is able to steer round corners. Another child is inside a tunnel which is being rocked by one of the staff. Ryan gets off the bike and joins him. They giggle together as the tunnel moves.

09.45   Ryan leaves the tunnel and walks towards a car. Another child also moves towards the car. Ryan starts to climb in but the other child pulls his coat from behind. Ryan turns and hits the boy who starts to cry. Ryan is told to go and sit down until he can behave. He hunches up on the seat and starts to chew his coat sleeve.

09.55   The children go in to wash their hands for snack time. Ryan enjoys playing with the water. He goes through into the area where the tables are set with mugs. He chooses one seat but when a member of staff sits down beside him, he turns his head and moves to the next seat. A jug of milk is passed round and the children help themselves. Ryan manages to pour out some milk which he drinks very quickly. He takes a biscuit, and when reminded, manages to say thank you although he doesn't look directly at the speaker.

10.10   The children have been talking about what they have been doing this morning. Ryan remembers he played with the bricks and went on the bike but only uses single words.

10.15   Ryan and his group are sitting at the table. The nursery nurse has brought a bowl of water and some objects and is explaining that they are going to see if the things are going to sink or float. Each child takes a turn to put something into the water. The answers are often guesses but they all have a try including Ryan. At the end of the session the children can choose what to do next. Ryan chooses to stay with the water.

10.45   Ryan is making quite a mess so the nursery nurse puts a cloth on the floor and stands the bowl on it. He continues to drop objects into the water. The nursery nurse decides to make notes about Ryan's ability to predict floating or sinking. He ignores her at first but does eventually answer and manages to get some of the answers right. He finishes with the water and goes over to the trays of toys. He takes the train set, tips it out onto the floor and starts to make a line of track. Another child comes over and makes a separate line. They continue independently. Occasionally Ryan puts a piece of track into his mouth and sucks it.

11.00   The children are warned that they have five more minutes before it is time to clear up. The track reaches across the floor, and staff and children have been stepping over it. A nursery nurse accidentally kicks a piece and Ryan scowls. He starts to throw pieces around. When asked to stop and begin clearing up he runs under the table.

11.15   A member of staff is sitting next to the table trying to coax Ryan out. When asked if he wants to come and listen to the story he shakes his head. Eventually he is persuaded to come out and sit on the mat, but he shuffles backwards away from the group. He is taken aside and asked why he is so cross today. He has his thumb in his mouth and just looks blankly.

At 11.30 Ryan is collected by his dad who asks 'Have you been good today?'

Evaluation

Ryan has good motor skills and can engage in imaginative play. His cognitive development is difficult to assess because of his language problems, but he did seem to have some understanding of floating and sinking.

Ryan plays alongside children but seldom interacts. He does not often make eye contact. He is still putting objects into his mouth.

Ryan is said to have 'a short fuse' and he reacts by throwing, pushing or hitting when upset. However observation showed that he did not always start the trouble.

Ryan starts school in six months' time and will find it very difficult with the larger groups and fewer adults. He is seeing the speech therapist now and has an appointment for assessment by the educational psychologist. The family are known to social services who have recently helped them to be rehoused, but they are still in high-rise accommodation.

Ryan has a lot of problems and may need to have learning support eventually but in the meantime what can you do to help?

1. Part of Ryan's problem may be that he has little opportunity to use up physical energy in the flat. He is rather boisterous so try to programme some physical activity before expecting him to sit and concentrate.

2. Discuss with your manager the possibility of a meeting with the speech therapist in order to plan activities which will encourage clearer speech, as part of the problem is Ryan's inability at times to make himself understood.

3. Encourage him to make more eye contact. This needs to be carefully managed so as not to appear threatening – maybe looking in mirrors first.

4. Try to distract him when he puts objects in his mouth by finding something interesting to do.

5. Encourage him to refrain from pushing and hitting by introducing a star chart for helpful behaviour, remembering that he is not always the instigator of the problem. Children quickly recognize that some members of the group are 'always in trouble' and this can lead to them being blamed for everything.

6. As with all children, you should be trying to 'catch him being good', and praising to reinforce the behaviour.

You will need to continue to monitor Colin and Ryan to see if there is any improvement. You will also need to work with your nursery team, the parents and other professionals in order to provide continuity.

Professionals you may meet as part of your role

Health Service

Family doctor (GP)

Everybody is entitled to be registered with a GP. Family doctors work in the community, sometimes alone but more usually as a member of a group practice. They are often based in a Health Centre with other professionals. Many centres have Well Person Clinics and Well Baby Clinics run in conjunction with the health visitor. Referrals are made to specialists and paramedical services if necessary.

Health Visitor

Health visitors are qualified nurses who have undertaken further specialist training in midwifery, child development and preventive medicine. They work exclusively in the community and are usually attached to a GP practice. They work mainly with the under-fives but may continue to support families who have special need. They routinely screen children for hearing and vision defects, and carry out developmental checks.

Physiotherapist

The majority of physios work in hospitals but some work in special schools or development assessment centres. They assess children's motor development and skills, and provide activities and exercises that parents and carers can use to encourage better mobility and co-ordination.

Occupational Therapist

Occupational therapists work in hospitals, residential schools and development assessment centres. They will make home/school visits if necessary in order to advise about specialist equipment to encourage independent life skills. They assess children's practical abilities and advise on the most appropriate activities.

Speech Therapist

Speech therapists may be employed in schools, in hospitals and in the community. They assess a child's speech, tongue and mouth movements, and understanding of language. They provide exercises and activities both to develop all aspects of children's spoken and receptive communication skills and to encourage language development.

Clinical Psychologist

Clinical psychologists are usually based in hospitals but some work from health centres. They assess children's social and emotional development and are often involved when children are said to have 'behavioural' difficulties. They often work with social services in planning pro-grammes at family centres.

Social Services

Social Worker

Most social workers now work in specialist teams such as those concerned with disability, the elderly and child protection. They support families and assess their needs. They are responsible for running family centres and for the registration of day nurseries and childminders. They are normally the prime worker when children are placed on 'at risk' registers or need court orders to protect them.

Family Centre Worker

They are trained nursery nurses who work with social services at family centres (previously day nurseries). The centres provide support for carers and children who are experiencing problems perhaps caused by disability or a perceived lack of parenting skills.

Education

Educational Psychologist

Educational psychologists are involved in the educational assessment of children with special needs. They use a battery of tests to try to establish these needs in order to prepare a statement of Special Educational Needs.

They act as advisors to professionals working directly with children who have a range of conditions which affect their ability to learn.

Special Educational Needs Co-ordinator (SENCO)

SENCOs advise teachers and support staff working with children who have been identified as having a special educational need. They also liaise with colleagues in special schools and with parents. They are responsible for co-ordinating provision for children including the IEP (individual education plan), for keeping the school's Special Education Needs (SEN) register and for working with external agencies.

Special Needs Teacher

Special needs teachers are qualified teachers with additional training and experience in working with children who have learning difficulties. They may work in a special school or be based in a unit in a mainstream school. There are also peripatetic teachers who visit children in mainstream schools. They may specialize in a particular disorder such as vision or hearing impairment.

Special Needs Support Assistant

Special needs support assistants work in both special and mainstream schools. They often work with individual statemented children, but are also involved with groups of children who are under-achieving. They usually work in the classroom under the direction of the teacher, but they also meet regularly with the SENCO to discuss planning. They may be qualified nursery nurses or undertake in-service training such as the Certificate in Learning Support.

5

Linking Observations and Assessments to the Desirable Outcomes for Learning

At the end of this chapter you will:

Have an awareness of the Desirable Outcomes for Learning.
Be able to use the outcomes' criteria to record children's progress and attainment.
Be able to use these records to inform curriculum planning, extend the children's experience and meet individual needs.
Understand more fully the partnership between parents and carers.

In January 1996 the School Curriculum and Assessment Authority (SCAA), in response to the government's request to consider the desirable outcomes for learning for children, published *Nursery Education: Desirable Outcomes for Children's Learning on Entering Compulsory Education*. This set of desirable outcomes was established for use in England as:

> goals for learning for children by the time they enter compulsory education. (Compulsory education begins the term after the child's fifth birthday.) They emphasise early literacy, numeracy and the development of personal and social skills, and contribute to children's knowledge, understanding and skills in other areas. Presented as six areas of learning, they provide a foundation for later achievement. (DfEE with SCAA, 1996)

The six areas of learning are:

- Personal and social development
- Language and literacy
- Mathematics
- Knowledge and understanding of the world
- Physical development
- Creative development

These areas provide a basis for the pre-school curriculum. They ensure that the curriculum being provided in pre-school establishments is appropriate for pre-school children. Any establishment wishing to receive government funding for 4-year-old children must be able to satisfy an OFSTED inspector that their setting will enable children to achieve the desirable outcomes by the time they are five years old.

Each area of learning has desirable outcomes which will provide a foundation for Key Stage 1 of the National Curriculum.

The outcomes for each area of learning follow, taken from DfEE with SCAA, 1996.

Personal and Social Development

Children are confident, show appropriate self-respect and are able to establish effective relationships with other children and with adults. They work as part of a group and independently, are able to concentrate and persevere in their learning and to seek help where needed. They are eager to explore new learning, and show the ability to initiate ideas and to solve simple practical problems. They demonstrate independence in selecting an activity or resources and in dressing and personal hygiene.

Children are sensitive to the needs and feelings of others and show respect for people of other cultures and beliefs. They take turns and share fairly. They express their feelings and behave in appropriate ways, developing an understanding of what is right, what is wrong and why. They treat living things, property and their environment with care and concern. They respond to relevant cultural and religious events and show a range of feelings, such as wonder, joy or sorrow, in response to their experiences of the world.

Language and Literacy

In small and large groups, children listen attentively and talk about their experiences. They use a growing vocabulary with increasing fluency to express thoughts and convey meaning to the listener. They listen and respond to stories, songs, nursery rhymes and poems. They make up their own stories and take part in role play with confidence.

Children enjoy books and handle them carefully, understanding how they are organised. They know that words and pictures carry meaning and that, in English, print is read from left to right and from top to bottom. They begin to associate sounds with patterns in rhymes, with syllables, and with words and letters. They recognise their own names and some familiar words. They recognise letters of the alphabet by shape and sound. In their writing they use pictures, symbols, familiar words and letters, to communicate meaning, showing awareness of some of the different purposes of writing. They write their names with appropriate use of upper and lower case letters.

Mathematics

Children use mathematical language, such as circle, in front of, bigger than and more, to describe shape, position, size and quantity. They recognise and recreate patterns. They are familiar with number rhymes, songs, stories, counting games and activities. They compare, sort, match, order, sequence and count using everyday objects. They recognise and use numbers to 10 and are familiar with larger numbers from their everyday lives. They begin to use their developing mathematical understanding to solve practical problems. Through practical activities children understand and record numbers, begin to show awareness of number operations, such as addition and subtraction, and begin to use the language involved.

Knowledge and Understanding of the World

Children talk about where they live, their environment, their families and past and present events in their own lives. They explore and recognise features of living things, objects and events in the natural and made world and look closely at similarities, differences, patterns and change. They show an awareness of the purposes of some features of the area in which they live. They talk about their observations, sometimes recording them and ask questions to gain information about why things happen and how things work. They explore and select materials and equipment and use skills such as cutting, joining, folding and building for a variety of purposes. They use technology, where appropriate, to support their learning.

Physical Development

Children move confidently and imaginatively with increasing control and co-ordination and an awareness of space and others. They use a range of small and large equipment and balancing and climbing apparatus, with increasing skill. They handle appropriate tools, objects, construction and malleable materials safely and with increasing control.

Creative Development

Children explore sound and colour, texture, shape, form and space in two and three dimensions. They respond in a variety of ways to what they see, hear, smell, touch and feel. Through art, music, dance, stories and imaginative play, they show an increasing ability to use their imagination, to listen and to observe. They use a widening range of materials, suitable tools, instruments and other resources to express ideas and to communicate their feelings.

How can these desirable outcomes be transposed into criteria suitable for the recording of children's progress and attainment, and then used to inform the future planning of the early years curriculum?

Since September 1998, schools in England and Wales have been using a formalized Baseline Assessment on each child shortly after the child has started statutory age schooling. These Baseline Assessments use the desirable outcomes criteria. A pre-school establishment should decide which record system will be manageable for them as a group and either design their own or use an already established format. Adults will need to consider how they assess children's learning and how effective their recording systems will be. Regular observation and assessment will enhance children's learning and development. Skilled observations of children can be utilized by staff, who should carefully analyse and evaluate the observation, recording the essential information regarding the child's progress and development. These observations of an individual child's development can then be used to help provide an appropriate curriculum for each child.

Records should contain accurate and up-to-date information about each child's development and progress. Each child's needs can be established and appropriate learning targets planned. The format for the record keeping should be easy to complete, relevant and accurate. The method chosen by a pre-school group should be consistent and agreed by all staff. Observations of each child should be undertaken about once every half-term, of more frequently if deemed necessary. This information can be used in three ways: to make a direct comparison with the child's development a few months ago; to make a comparison with child development 'norms'; to record the child's progress in attaining the desirable outcomes for learning. Whichever reason is decided on, it is important that the observation be promptly recorded, legible, dated, and signed. Prepared sheets are helpful. Remember that these notes are confidential. Clearly, when the observations are written up, these should be made available to the child's parents or carers. It is, however, useful to discuss your observations with your colleagues, especially if you have particular concerns or if you suspect that you have not recognized and described your prior assumptions. Parents should be given the opportunity to contribute to assessments. Parents should be informed of the written format of the records that are regularly used by the setting. This will enable them to contribute more easily and readily to the assessment of their child. See pp. 98–100 on the partnership with parents.

Good record keeping enables a setting to:

- Assess and record what a child has learnt in relation to the criteria for the Desirable Outcomes for Learning and/or Key Stage 1 of the National Curriculum.

- Assess and record the stage of development the child has reached.

- Plan a balanced curriculum, based on the needs of the child. Plan continuity and progression for each child. These next stages must be based on a knowledge and understanding of individual children's experience and understanding.

- Identify any special educational needs and formulate an individual educational plan if necessary.

Partnerships with Parents: Ways of Sharing Information

Parents are a valuable resource when assessing a child's development. They know a great deal about their own children. They have background information that will have a definite impact on how the child works through a variety of experiences and environments. As children often behave in a manner that has a direct link to the home environment it makes sense to use this valuable resource.

Many factors will influence how we do this in order to achieve what is best for the families and their individual children. There will always be a variety of styles and levels of parenting, and a great variation in the levels of interest shown in children's education. Parents are concerned about the quality of care and education their children are receiving, but some feel it is totally the teacher's role to 'educate'. These tend to be confident in the care being given and the level of learning achieved. A positive inspection report is all they need to affirm their faith in the school. They only become involved if there is a problem. Other parents like to follow their child's progress carefully and to be involved in every aspect of their development and learning. They visit often, volunteer for a variety of tasks and attend meetings.

There are also parents who would like to be more involved, but are overwhelmed or alienated by institutions and schools. Staff may mistakenly interpret their non-attendance at school functions and meetings as due to a lack of interest. It is also essential to schedule meetings when parents (particularly working parents) can attend. The provision of crèche facilities for younger siblings should be included in meeting announcements. The goal is to establish and maintain partnerships with *all* parents.

We should all have the same aim: **to help the child develop and**

extend their learning. To achieve this we need to share experiences and information about the child. How can this be accomplished? Here are some suggestions:

- Take every opportunity to chat informally with parents.
- Keep a brief record so that you know which parents you haven't talked to recently, and which parents are taking up most of your time.
- Share information passed on by parents with other members of staff. Some of this information may be very important to the child's welfare but may not be formally recorded, for example a father's absence or a grandmother's illness.
- Plan an area where children, parents and staff can display photographic evidence of a variety of events and activities. These can be used for the group or individual photo albums – a year book that everyone involved with the child can contribute to. Special events can be videoed and loaned to parents. This requires careful organization but an interested parent might be willing to do this. Older children might take it on as a project in the design and technology curriculum. Regular 'feature films' on school life could be just the thing to attract parents into the classroom.

Pastoral care is a very important area to consider. Parents are happy when things are going well. We need to help them to support children when things are not as satisfactory. Educational progress is important, but when parents feel pressurized by other parents, teachers or the media about their child's ability to read, for example, it puts extra strain on the family and this is not helpful to the child. We must find a reporting format that provides an up-to-date record of achievement, but does not reinforce competition and comparison. It is essential that parents know the nursery and school expectations, how they can support and encourage their children, and who to go to for help if there is a problem.

We also need to ask ourselves if families are made to feel comfortable with all aspects of the school environment. Have their family structures been accommodated by the establishment: their cultures, languages, religious beliefs? Do we check with parents what they really want or do we decide first what we expect and then assume that parents will follow our guidelines? If parents do not conform and do not seem interested, have we asked them the reason for this? Does the school programme positively reflect the cultural, language and faith diversity of the families? Are the school guidelines discussed and negotiated with parents? Do school staff make planned and energetic attempts to involve all parents, rather than automatically assuming lack of interest?

Here are a few of the many innovative ways that have been devised to make possible partnerships with all parents:

- Provide a family room where parents can meet, relax and share experiences and where teachers can drop in for an informal chat.
- Plan a workshop on the way reading is taught in the school. This can inform parents about useful ways to help their children at home.
- Encourage parents to stay and watch the children working on occasion so that they can understand the aims and objectives of the teaching. Provide an outline of the term activities and how parents and other family members might help.
- Invite parents to contribute ideas and objects for displays linked to the area. Families who have lived locally for several years will enjoy the opportunity to contribute to a school project. It may foster a greater sense of belonging amongst newcomers.
- Involve parents in decisions about the topics and timing of open days, parents' evenings and workshops in order to enable as many as possible to attend.

Diagrams and Practical Materials to Support the Book

Charts and diagrams can be down-loaded from the Cassell web site and copied without charge.

Go to: www.cassell-prof.co.uk

These charts and diagrams provide useful examples for the development of your own observation and record-keeping systems.

6

Activities to Promote Developmental Progress

The main reason we observe children is to see what they are able to do and then lead them forward. In Chapter 3 examples of observations were given with evaluations which often suggested activities that would help children overcome a difficulty or perfect a skill. For example, if a child has difficulty cutting out with scissors then we would provide exercises to strengthen finger muscles and opportunities to practise. If children lack concentration we would develop games and activities to help their listening skills and maintain their interest. If they have problems integrating into a new setting we would think about ways to interest them in working first with one member of staff and then in a small group. In each case the activities we provide would come about as the result of carefully observing the children in order to assess their needs.

The activities which follow have been arranged in age progression so that they allow you to think about adapting them to individual children. The age headings are only guidelines. They have been grouped into areas of development which relate to NVQ competences but of course they can be used in your everyday practice.

The lists are certainly not definitive. They are meant to trigger your own thoughts about providing valuable experiences for the children in your care.

DEVELOPMENTAL AREA – MOTOR SKILLS

C 3.2 Develop children's skills of locomotion and balance

Age group 0–1 year

Offer an *adult grasp* to encourage a baby to help herself up. Encourage baby to feel her feet and bounce up and down while in the adult grasp. Allow baby to *kick freely* whenever possible.
Give baby an opportunity to *crawl* at 9 months.
Assist standing – allowing the child to *pull to stand*.
Encourage the year-old child to *walk around* the playpen and provide opportunities for safe supported walking, such as with push-along toys, e.g. trolley with bricks.

Age group 1–4 years

Continue to provide toys that will assist walking.
Encourage toddlers' mobility by providing balls to run after.
Wriggling – organize children in a circle and ask them to wriggle finger-tips, then wrists, arms and finally make arms into windmills. Wriggle toes, ankles, knees and finally shake the legs.
Stretching and curling – ask children to find a space and lie on the floor. Ask them to stretch their bodies and curl up again. Repeat stretching in a different direction and curling up in a different manner.
Walking and running – ask children to walk slowly around the room, moving in and out of each other but not bumping. Increase the pace to jogging and then running as fast as possible. Slow down gradually. Ask the children to walk backwards without bumping into each other.

Age group 4–8 years

The same activities as for younger children but with increased skill.
Follow My Leader – set out a few pieces of equipment, such as balancing bars, hoops and coiled ropes, for the children to avoid. Ask the children to follow you with the music and move around the room leaping, jump-ing, turning and hopping. Use large, exaggerated movements. Then allow the child behind you to take the lead.
Outdoor/indoor activity circuit – lay out hoops, skipping ropes, balanc-ing bars, tunnels and slides and supervise the children as they go round the circuit. (N.B. The younger the children, the more adults will be required to supervise.)

C 3.3   Develop children's gross motor skills

Age group 0–1 year

Babies under 1 year old are unlikely to be throwing, catching or playing games involving bat and ball, but the skills encouraged in the locomotion and balance area will assist.

Age group 1–4 years

Young children love to throw things and this can be channelled into a game using a ball.

They also like to try to catch a ball but at the age of 2 to 3 the ball needs to be quite large and thrown into the child's arms.

A *catch circle game* can be introduced at nursery age. Form a small group of children into a circle, then stand in the middle and throw a variety of large balls and bean bags to the children to encourage catching and throwing skills.

Age group 4–8 years

A *catch circle*. As with the younger children but using smaller balls, smaller bean bags, bats and frisbees. This can be done in the circle or with children working together in pairs.

Team games involving bats, like rounders and cricket, can be introduced as the children reach 7, but such games take a lot of practice, and not all children will be very successful.

C 3.4 Develop children's fine motor skills

Age group 0–1 year

Mobiles and *pram beads* should be placed near the baby to encourage reaching out to feel.

Encourage the 6–12-month-old baby to play with nesting cubes and beakers, large beads, floating bath toys, plastic saucepans and lids, and cotton reels.

Activity centres with different actions which the baby can move.

Age group 1–4 years

Finger painting, Play-doh, hand printing.
Construction toys, such as Lego, wooden blocks, Stickle Bricks.
Spatter painting, fruit/vegetable printing, cutting and glueing.
Junk modelling.
Simple puppet making: paper bag puppets
　　　　　　　　　　　cereal box puppets
　　　　　　　　　　　sock puppets
　　　　　　　　　　　paper plate puppets
　　　　　　　　　　　wooden spoon puppets.
Table-top toys like jigsaws, mosaics, large bead threading.
Action nursery rhymes like 'Tommy Thumb'.

Age group 4–8 years

Junk modelling.
Crayon resist patterns.
Cutting and glueing – collage.
Puppet making.
Drawing, clay modelling, stencilling.
Paper folding, paper weaving, sewing.
More complex construction kits such as Meccano.
More complicated jigsaw puzzles and mosaics.

> C 1   Level 2 Support children's physical development needs
>
> C 3   Level 3 Promote the physical development of children

Age group 0–1 year

Allow a baby to *kick freely* whenever possible.
Give the baby the opportunity to *roll* safely.
Encourage a baby of 6 months to bounce up and down while being held.
Assist the 9-month child to pull to stand by providing strong support.
Encourage the baby to *crawl* by placing a variety of interesting objects close by.
Encourage the year-old child to *walk* by providing opportunities to do so in safety and with suitable equipment, e.g. push/pull-along toys.

Age group 1–4 years

Allow plenty of time for play in the bath.
Encourage the child·to walk with reins when they are able.
Allow toddlers to walk round the furniture safely.
Provide large balls.
Play games like Ring O' Roses.
Provide access to large mobile toys like tricycles, wheelbarrows, dolls' prams.
Provide access to safe climbing toys at playgroup or the park.

Age group 4–8 years

This is a very active period in children's lives. They will normally exercise freely without much help from adults.
Provide safe, supervised areas for children to run, climb, balance, dance, etc.
Encourage children to refine their movements during organized games and PE sessions.
Be aware that some children have difficulty with balance and provide activities which will assist this.

DEVELOPMENTAL AREA – LANGUAGE SKILLS

C11 Promote children's language and communication development

Age group 0–1 year

Talk and listen to the baby so that they learn speech is a two-way process.

Encourage listening skills by providing musical toys.

Introduce repetitive rhymes and songs – reinforced by actions.

Towards the end of the first year introduce simple picture books with one illustration to the page of familiar objects like cup, ball, teddy. You can also make your own book using photographs of family and objects from around the home.

Name parts of the body as you dress and undress the baby.

Age group 1–4 years

Continue talking and listening about everyday activities.

When saying nursery rhymes, stop before the last word to give the toddler a chance to complete it.

Sing naming rhymes, e.g. 'Tommy Thumb', 'This is the way we nod our head, brush our teeth, etc'.

Introduce action songs like 'The wheels on the bus go round and round'.

Encourage listening skills with tapes and story books – especially those with repetition, like *The Enormous Turnip* and *The Very Hungry Caterpillar*, or any favourite stories including those made up to include the child's name. (NB The names of the participants pulling up the turnip and the foods that the caterpillar eats can be adapted to names within the child's experience.)

Provide dressing-up clothes for role-play language.

Age group 4–8 years

Talk and listen to the children, using open-ended questions.

Introduce songs that the children can join in or make up for themselves.

Create opportunities for imaginative play, e.g. puppet theatres, home corners set up as shops, cafes, hospitals, hairdressers, etc.

Encourage an interest in books that gradually have more complicated plots and characters.

Encourage listening skills with games like Simon Says and Musical Statues, or identifying noises in a bingo quiz where the children listen to a tape of animal or household noises.

Play games like I Spy which make the children think about the sounds that letters make.

Label objects so that the child will recognize that written symbols stand for words.

Encourage children to write their own stories and letters – these can be recorded on tape if writing skills are not well developed.

Introduce children to poetry and rhymes. Have them write their own.

Make children think about language by making up riddles, e.g.

> This is a word that rhymes with *up*,
> you can drink out of me because I'm a (*cup*).

> I'm brown and I'm hard, I grow in the *ground*.
> When you've cooked me and peeled me, I'm soft, white and *round*. (potato)

Have a 'Round the World Week' where the children learn how to write the words for Hello and Goodbye in as many languages as possible in order to understand the concept of symbols standing for meaning. This can also be extended into sign language and picture language, e.g. the willow pattern plate telling a story, or tracking signs.

DEVELOPMENTAL AREA – SENSORY AWARENESS

C 10.2   Develop children's awareness and understanding of sensory experiences

Age group 0–1 year

Touch
Stroke the baby.
Gently tickle and blow across the chest when changing the nappy.
Lay the baby on a sheepskin, or a textured blanket, etc. and allow to explore with hands and feet.
Provide textured balls, cubes, etc. to play with.
Allow baby to play with safe kitchen implements, such as plastic bowls and wooden spoons.
Allow baby to finger-feed in order to feel the different textures of food.

Taste
Introduce different foods during weaning.

Smell
Bathtime.
Food.

Sight
Provide mobiles for the baby in the cot or pram.
Roll balls and other toys in front of the child.
Place pictures near the baby for him/her to focus on.
Play Peek-a-boo.

Hearing
Sing to the baby.
Rattles and musical toys.

Age group 1–4 years

Touch
Provide an activity centre, textured book or mat.
Allow to play in sand, water and with Play-doh.
Experiment with finger painting.
Allow children to help with cooking and food preparation and to feel the different textures.

Taste
Try out new foods.

Smell
Cookery activities.
Bathtime.
Gardening – flowers, vegetables.

Sight
Widen the child's experience of the world by visiting new places, e.g. the park, the zoo, the seaside.
Introduce books that gradually have more complicated pictures.
Introduce the child to the new images on television.

Hearing
Encourage the child to listen by telling stories.
Help sound discrimination by playing games which require the children to move at different speeds.
Play simple sound recognition games, like identifying the sounds well-known animals make.

Age group 4–8 years

Touch
Feel objects in a box which are simple to identify but become increasingly difficult.

Sort into sets objects which are hard/soft, warm/cold.

Texture picture making: provide corrugated paper, shiny and tissue paper, feathers, pasta, etc.

Bread making.

Textures in the environment – tree bark, stones, grass, etc.

Taste

Try out different foods when learning about other countries.

Blindfold taste experiments.

Smell

Treasure boxes with scented soaps, children's perfume.

Cookery activities – especially those using herbs.

Blindfold smelling experiments.

Gardening.

Sight

Drawing from life.

Describing objects in the room for the other children to guess.

Provide more complicated pictures – perhaps with a person or objects hidden in them.

Spot-the-differences pictures.

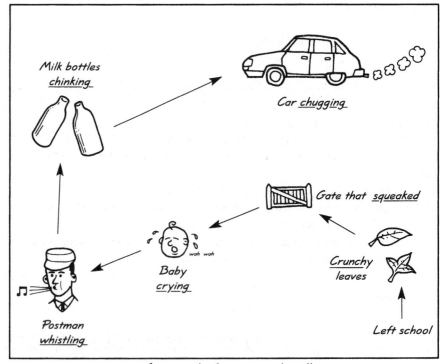

Figure 6.1   *A record of our sound walk*

Hearing
Moving to music.
Playing in a band.
Spot That Tune.

Sound walks that the children record when they get back. (See Figure 6.1.)

DEVELOPMENTAL AREA – COGNITIVE SKILLS

C 10.3 Develop children's understanding of mathematics and science

Age group 0–1 year

Talk about everyday objects like the *blue* ball, the *green* trousers, the *red* bus.
Sing 'number' rhymes: 'Ten little toes – one little nose'.
'1, 2, 3, 4, 5 – once I caught a fish alive'.
Count the stairs as you climb up.
Provide toys which are brightly coloured and have different textures and shape for the baby to explore with mouth and then fingers.
Play games like 'Round and round the garden, like a teddy bear'.

Age group 1–4 years

Provide building blocks of different colours that the toddler can build *up* and knock *down*.
Play action games and rhymes: Ring-O'-Roses.
Sorting exercises, like putting socks and shoes into pairs, clearing up toys into the right boxes.
If the child has a zoo or farmyard – put all the animals of one sort together. (This can lead to talking about big and small if the animals have young.)
Play simple matching games like Picture Dominoes.
Introduce action songs with counting:
'Five little ducks went swimming one day'.
'Five currant buns in the baker's shop' (this can be any food).
'Five little speckled frogs sat on a speckled log'.
(NB These are useful because they allow the child to start learning about subtraction.)

Age group 4–8 years

Help concepts of volume by providing water play with jugs and beakers of various sizes.

Help concepts of mass by providing sand and Play-doh which can be 'shared out'.

Help concepts of time by setting up friezes that show things we do when we: get up, eat our breakfast, go to school, etc.

Sequencing activities – e.g. size.

> Grow beans or sunflowers and plot their growth. (See Figure 6.2.)
>
> Talk about and display frogspawn – tadpole – baby frog – adult frog.
>
> Have a display showing baby – toddler – child – adult.

(Sequencing also helps left to right orientation – a prerequisite for reading.)

Sorting into different property sets, e.g. things that float or sink, those that are attracted by a magnet and those that are not.

Introduce games with a scoring system that require the child first to add on, then take away and finally multiply.

Figure 6.2 'Grow beans or sunflowers and plot their growth.'

A record of our sunflower

DEVELOPMENTAL AREA – SOCIAL AND EMOTIONAL

> *C 4.3   Level 2 Help children to develop self-reliance and self-esteem*

> *C 5.3   Level 3 Develop children's self-reliance and self-esteem.*

These are areas that should be thought about whenever you are working with children. The activities you provide if you have carried out observations should be challenging, but not so far beyond the child's capabilities that they do not have the chance to succeed and feel good about themselves.

Age group 0–1 year

Activities that will help the baby feel positive about themself – smiling, playing Peek-a-boo, cuddling, answering back when they attempt to communicate.
Provide a mirror for babies to see how they look.
After 6 months allow the baby to finger-feed in safety.
At 9 months allow the baby to hold a spoon at mealtimes – although do not expect success at this age.

Age group 1–4 years

Continue to allow to finger-feed and hold a spoon, which should become more successful by 18 months.
Promote dressing skills by making a doll, book, etc. that will give practice at doing up buttons, buckles, zips and any other fastenings familiar to the child's mode of dress.
Provide clothing and utensils in the home corner which will reflect the child's home life and show that it is valued.

Age group 4–8 years

Allow sufficient time before and after a physical training session for the children to undress and dress by themselves.
Have a dressing-up race where children put on hats, gloves, etc.
Preparing and sharing a meal – this can be sandwiches at 4 years and gradually become more elaborate. (Try out recipes from around the world.)
Team building and working together can be improved by providng challenges which require co-operation. This can be to build a railway at 4 or a lighthouse with working parts at 8.
Display all of the children's work at some time so that they can share in the praise.

DEVELOPMENTAL AREA – IMAGINATIVE SKILLS

C 9.3   Level 2 Select and use equipment and materials to stimulate role play

C 10.4   Level 3 Develop children's imagination and creativity

Age group 1–4 years

Allow toddler to imitate housework, driving the car, cooking, shopping.
Provide dressing-up props, such as hats and lengths of cloth.
Provide boxes, large blocks, etc. that can be used to make houses, buses, boats.
In nursery have a corner which can be screened off to provide an intimate home area where the children can relax and act out their stories. If possible, provide utensils and decorations which reflect the home lives of all the children in the nursery.
In order to stimulate the interest and add to the language of the rising 4-year-olds this area can be changed into other familiar settings, such as a café or shop. If you have a friendly dentist you could obtain a supply of stickers, posters, etc. in order to set up a role-play situation which could allay children's fears.
Where possible, the outdoor area should contain large apparatus like a climbing frame and trolleys which can provide the necessary stimulus for adventure play, as well as improving physical skills.

Age group 4–8 years

The 4- and 5-year-old will still enjoy a home corner, which can be extended further into a garage, hairdresser's, doctor's surgery or post office.
Allow the children to make fruit, vegetables, food for a café out of salt dough which can be baked, painted and varnished to last longer.
Children can make masks and costumes in order to engage in dramatic play – this can be extended to a class production of a story.

7

Developmental Milestones from Birth to 8 Years

In previous chapters we discussed how to carry out observations in different formats. We considered how the knowledge we gained could help children to progress and how the activities we provided could lead a child forward. As part of the process of evaluation it was also pointed out that it is necessary to compare your findings with what we expect children to be doing at different stages.

In Chapter 3 there are references to the work of Mary Sheridan, Catherine Lee, Patricia Geraghty, Valda Reynolds and Jean Piaget. There are many books written about the progress of children's development, and it is important that you read a good selection. However, to enable you to start your observation collection we have included a summary of developmental milestones to which you may refer.

As stated many times, though, you must take into consideration the fact that children differ in quite normal ways. All children follow the same sequence of growth and development, but the rate varies from child to child. Each aspect of development is affected by the environment in which the child is placed and the experiences they encounter. No two children, even though living in the same material environment, will have exactly the same experiences, or will be affected by them in exactly the same way. Every child is unique and will progress at their own individual rate. However, if we want to provide the best opportunities to encourage the child's development we must know broadly what to expect of him/her at each stage, so that we can provide the right environment. In this way we would hope to meet the needs of children and allow them to reach their full potential. To illustrate the sequence of development we have first included flow charts of developmental areas, and indicated in some instances the way that environmental factors may influence them.

The child is a whole person and all aspects of development go on simultaneously, but observations often concentrate on one area, so the age-related guide which follows is arranged under five headings: physical, intellectual, language, social and emotional. For ease of writing and reference the stages have also been arranged in whole years from the age of 3. The reader will need to bear in mind that we would not expect a child of 4 years 1 month to be at the same stage as a child of 4 years 11 months.

Students often hope to find that the behaviour they observe will be referred to in exactly the same language in the reference book. This is not always the case; you may need to adapt the skill to another situation. For example, if it mentions a child's ability to build bricks you could compare it with a child building tin cans or books. You may also need to look back or forwards to see if the skill has been mentioned in a different age group. This is particularly true in the physical section, where abilities cannot be mentioned every time.

Lastly, it must be noted that most of the observations and developmental stages are based on the writers' experiences of working with children in England. There will be variations in the cultural and social expectations of children which may affect the way in which they develop. The knowledge for compiling the stages comes from observing children over many years and reflects many different experiences. They are not based on any standardized results, such as those used to compile growth charts or Sheridan's (1995) developmental stages, but they obviously reflect some of the learning undertaken by the writers during their own training. This is particularly true for Carole Sharman, whose work as a health visitor involved screening children for any developmental delay using first Mary Sheridan's guidelines, and then the Denver Developmental Screening Test. The Denver guidelines were standardized in America, as the name suggests, and do reflect the different ethnic groups that make up the population. All the authors have worked with nursery and school-aged children before teaching on the Nursery Nurse courses in Further Education, and they continue to observe children when visiting student placements. The guidelines therefore reflect as up-to-date abilities as is possible. (See Figures 7.1 to 7.5.)

Figure 7.1 Developmental areas.

Key features

Supporting role
of adult carer

	Key features	Supporting role of adult carer
1 – 6 months	Responds to primary carer. Can swing from pleasure to displeasure and vice versa quickly. Cries when uncomfortable, hungry or lonely. Shows eagerness and anger vocally. Generally friendly.	Provide regular, routine care in a secure and stable environment. Provide a basis of love. Provide consistent care.
6 – 9 months	Becoming anxious with strangers. Shows annoyance and anger by kicking legs and screaming. Begins to show patience when waiting for preparation of familiar things.	A safe, secure environment for sitting and crawling and the companionship of adults. Provide love and affection. Give praise and encouragement.
9 – 18 months	Growing independence can lead to rage when thwarted. Shows anxiety when left alone. Emotionally more stable but can be jealous of adults' attention to other children. Can be defiant – learns NO.	Encourage independence and confidence. Give positive messages to child to encourage self-esteem. Value each child for what they are. Demonstrate consistent attitudes to behaviour and discipline.
18 months – 3 years	Increased independence brings strong emotional feelings. Anger and frustration can lead to tantrums. Can be very loving and affectionate. Calmer as third birthday approaches – less likely to have tantrums.	Help children to relate to each other. Set out consistent boundaries for behaviour and give reasonable guidelines for what is acceptable.
3 – 5 years	Very co-operative and friendly. Copies attitudes and moods of adults. More stable and emotionally secure. Shows purpose and persistence, and control over emotions.	Needs support and reassurance when begins nursery. Give adult approval regularly, as children enjoy this. Provide activities which allow the child to succeed.
5 – 7 years	Confident and independent. Can boast and show off. Decides to excel in every thing that is undertaken. Good control of emotions. 6-year-old less stable and swings from love to hate.	Needs support in difficult situations. Provide activities which reflect positive images of all children regardless of ethnic background, disability or gender.

Figure 7.2 Emotional development.

Figure 7.3 Physical development.

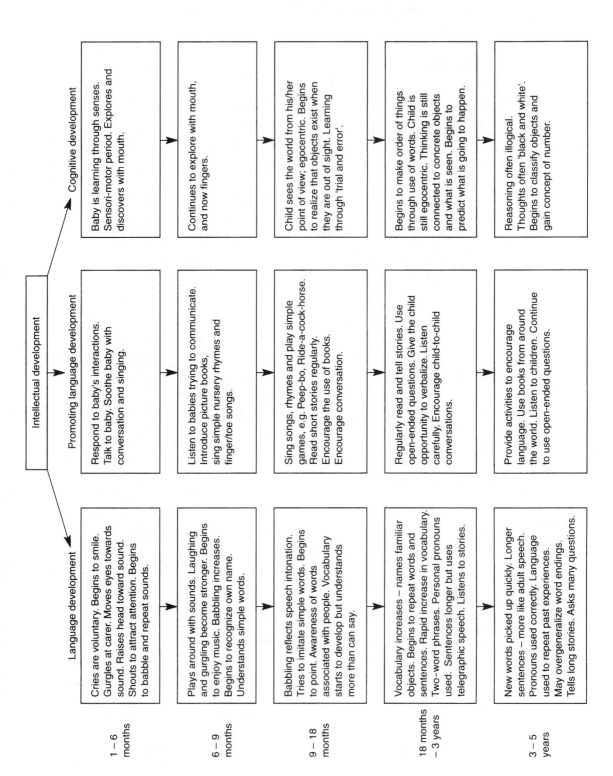

Figure 7.4 Intellectual, language and cognitive development.

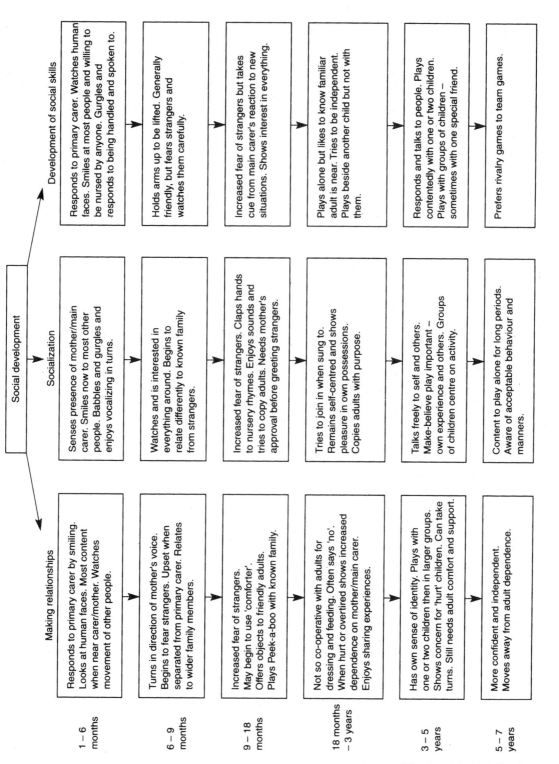

Figure 7.5 Social development.

The neonate

At birth infants are totally dependent on an adult to meet their needs for protection, love and food. Their movements are mainly reflex, although the latest research suggests babies are able to 'copy' certain gestures soon after delivery. They communicate their needs by crying.

Physical development

The body of a full-term baby is rounded and on average weighs 3.4 kg. Length is around 45–50 cm. The head is large in proportion to the body.

Pulled to sitting position, the head falls back, but held upright under the arms the shoulders support the head for a few seconds before giving way. Placed on their stomach (prone), the head turns to one side and the legs are drawn up under the abdomen.

On their back (supine) the head is to one side and the arm on that side is extended – if the head is turned round to the other side then that arm will extend (tonic neck reflex).

Other reflexes present at birth but which will disappear in 6–8 weeks are: Moro/startle, rooting, sucking, grasp, walking, stepping.

Sight – turns to light, sharp visual field at 25–30 cm.

Hearing acute – turns to sound, responds to voice, especially female pitch.

Smell and taste sensitive – recognizes mother's milk, responds to nice and 'nasty' smells.

Touch response strong – many of the reflexes are a response to touch. Babies will often be comforted by touch and it is thought to be a major factor in the bonding process.

Sleeps about 21 hours a day.

Intellectual development

Sucking gives pleasure and baby learns to recognize the sights and sounds of feeding.

Has been shown to concentrate on faces and imitate – yawn, tongue poking.

Language development

Communicates needs by crying, which can often be distinguished by main carer as indicating hunger, tiredness, boredom, pain or discomfort.

Grunts and snuffles with satisfaction.
Will often 'still' to a continuous, moderately loud, adult voice.

Social and emotional development

Totally dependent on adults.
Responds to nursing but does not like to be over-handled.
Likes to sleep but very alert when awake.

Three months old

Babies are awake for longer periods and are beginning to understand more about themselves and the wider environment. Their actions and language have become more deliberate.

Physical development

Actions are more controlled and purposeful. Early reflexes have disappeared.
Supine, lies with head in mid-line and there is little or no head lag when pulled up to sitting.
Held in the sitting position, the back is straighter except in the lumbar region.
Kicks very vigorously but if held in the standing position the legs tend to sag at the knees.
Waves hand symmetrically and will bring hands together across the chest to hold a rattle momentarily.
When placed in the prone position will lift up onto forearms to have a look round.
Visually alert – follows a moving object around and will stare at a still object for a few seconds.
Watches own hands very closely and plays with fingers.
The defensive blink reflex is now present.
Turns head and eyes to locate a sound but upset by very loud noises.
May be sleeping through the night and awake for longer periods after a feed.

Intellectual development

Recognizes familiar sounds and objects, like the bath running or feed arriving, and shows excitement by kicking legs and vocalizing. Has learned that calling out brings attention and relief.

Language development

Vocalizes loudly. Coos and squeals with pleasure.
Takes turns in conversations with adults.

Social development

Responds to handling with smiles and gurgles.
Friendly towards any interested adult or child. Enjoys games with them.

Emotional development

Less self-centred and reacts more to the surroundings, but dislikes sudden loud noises and cries when uncomfortable or annoyed. Still very dependent on familiar adults for reassurance and care.

Six months old

Babies now begin to explore more with their hands. Better eye–hand co-ordination allows them to reach out and grasp objects. They are learning that they are separate from their environment.

Physical development

On back, raises head and lifts legs to grasp hold of feet.
When placed on stomach, lifts head and chest well up, supporting self on flattened palms and outstretched arms.
Can sit with support and turn round to look at their surroundings.
Moves hands and arms purposefully and will hold out arms to be picked up.
When pulled into a sitting position will help by bracing the shoulders.
Held to stand, can support own weight and loves to bounce up and down.
Kicks strongly with alternating feet. Able to roll over from back to front.
Picks up toys using whole hand (palmar grasp) and can pass from hand to hand.
Explores everything with their mouth.
First teeth may appear. Able to chew and usually taking solids well.

Intellectual development

Beginning to react to strange people or situations.
Will watch where a toy falls if it is within visual field but forgets it if it disappears.
Beginning to understand cause and effect, e.g. rattle makes noise if shaken.
Smiles at own image in mirror. Will imitate for effect, e.g. coughing.

Language development

Uses voice tunefully, making sing-song vowel sounds or single or double syllables like la-la, da-da, u-u, ga-ga, ah-ah. Laughs, chuckles and squeals with delight or annoyance.

Social development

Sleeps less and wants more company to play with.
Often still friendly towards strangers but beginning to be shy or anxious when approached, especially if main carer is out of sight.

Emotional development

Still very reliant on main carer and familiar people and surroundings, but beginning to show more independence. Becoming more of a personality.

Nine months old

Babies at this age are now becoming mobile. Crawling, shuffling, creeping and rolling extends their world. Finer finger control allows more detailed exploration of that world.

Physical development

Moving around the floor.
Pulls self up to stand, using furniture, people, etc. and will stand holding on. However, lets go and falls backwards with a bump.
Held standing, will walk forward.
Sits unsupported for long periods of time and can lean forward to reach a toy without overbalancing.
Uses a crude thumb and index finger (pincer) grasp to pick up small objects and pokes with index finger.
Tries to take the spoon when being fed. Finger-feeds well.

Intellectual development

Very interested in surroundings. When exploring, shows great determination and curiosity.
Still examines things with mouth.
Will search for toys that go out of sight.
Imitates clapping and waving bye-bye with some understanding of meaning.

Language development

Uses voice deliberately. Shouts for attention.
Babbles tunefully: dad-dad-dad, mum-mum-mum. This is largely for baby's own amusement but also a sign of ability to recognize main carers.
Imitates sounds and converses in a two-way conversation.
Understands 'No' and 'Bye-bye'.

Social development

Happy and sociable with familiar adults and children but may be shy of strangers. This will be shown by clinging to carer and hiding their face.
Attracts attention by shouting or crawling over and pulling clothing of an adult.
May play Pat-a-cake or Peek-a-boo.

Emotional development

Babies have really become attached to their families and depend on them for reassurance. Because they are secure in their love they have become more aware of strangers.
Increasingly seeking independence, they will throw themselves backwards and stiffen in annoyance if they cannot do what they want to.

One year old

The horizontal positional of the new-born has now given way to the vertical position of the 1-year-old, struggling to learn to walk. Use of language is growing and they are enthusiastic in experimenting with their limited adult's vocalizations.

Physical development

Sits very well and can sit up from lying down unaided. Usually crawling or bottom shuffling very fast.
Pulls to standing, using furniture, but collapses with a bump on letting go. Walks sideways around the furniture. Walks with hand held. May stand alone for a few seconds.
May crawl upstairs (average 13–14 months).
Picks up small objects with neat pincer grasp (between thumb and tip of index finger).

Feeding skills: can hold cup and drink with a little assistance. Holds spoon but unable to feed self.
Helps with dressing, e.g. holding out arm for sleeve.
May only have one sleep during the day.

Intellectual development

Explores objects with mouth less often.
Drops and throws toys and watches them fall, then looks in the correct area when they roll out of sight.
Likes to look out of the window and watch cars, people, etc.
Beginning to show an interest in pictures in books. Knows own name and responds to it.
Imitates a great deal. Enjoys sounds and will experiment with toys that make a noise.

Language development

Babbles loudly, tunefully and incessantly. Understands simple commands, e.g. come to mummy/daddy.
May say two or three words (nouns) with meaning, e.g. mummy, daddy, sibling or pet's name, but understands many more.

Social development

Inclined to be shy with strangers – likes to be able to see and hear a familiar adult.
Enjoys an audience and will repeat acts that are laughed at. Plays Pat-a-cake and waves good-bye.

Emotional development

Capable of primitive affection and jealous of main carer's attention.
Developing a degree of independence as mobility increases but need to feel they can explore and then return for security.
Demonstrate a growing need for independence in their struggle to feed themselves.

Fifteen months old

The baby is a toddler now. They are usually walking and, although unsteady, are very proud of the fact. Their mobility and increasing curiosity makes this period an exciting but often frustrating time.

Demands on their carer are increased as toddlers become more daring in their explorations. They have to learn self-discipline and adapt to social demands, and this can result in negative behaviour over the next two years.

Physical development

Walks alone with feet wide apart, using arms outstretched to help balance. Can get to feet alone and launch self forward, but progress is limited by falling or bumping into furniture.
Lets self down by collapsing backwards but may fall forwards into crawling position.
Crawls upstairs and can kneel to play with toys.
Can push a large truck along but has no control over where it goes.
Picks up small objects with a precise pincer grasp.
Holds a crayon with a palmar grasp and makes a mark on the paper if shown.
Holds two building blocks and may put one on top of the other.
Assists with dressing. Can bring spoon to mouth and obtain some food before turning the spoon over.
Not able to throw yet, so just drops (casts) toys.

Intellectual development

Less likely to explore with mouth now and uses fingers instead.
Points at familiar toys and objects when asked.
Intensely curious about everything around – people, objects and events, likes going out for trips.
Does not associate dolls with being a baby – will carry them by an arm, leg or hair.

Language development

Jabbers loudly and continuously with sounds becoming more complex.
Can say about two to six recognizable words but understands many more, e.g. will respond to simple requests and point to something they want.
Recognizes familiar songs, rhymes and TV tunes.

Social development

Enjoys familiar company and loves fuss and attention.
Attempts to join in games and rhymes.

Emotional development

Begins a period of emotional unsteadiness. May become negative and refuse to co-operate, or do the opposite of what is asked. Temper tantrums are not uncommon until the age of 3.
Very dependent on adults for reassurance.

Eighteen months old

Children are gaining skill and confidence in movement (see Figure 7.6) and gradually adding to their vocabulary and understanding of the world. Emotionally they are still very dependent on the main carer and need a lot of affection and reassurance. If they are allowed to be dependent at this stage they will develop the stability and feeling of self-worth that will enable them to be confident in the future.

Figure 7.6 Eighteen months old. Children are gaining skill and confidence in movements.

Physical development

Walks well without needing to hold out arms for balance.
Can stoop to pick up toys from the floor without falling over.
Walks upstairs holding on, but crawls down.
Pushes and pulls (walking backwards) large, wheeled toys but cannot steer round obstacles.
Climbs onto chair and then turns round to sit.
Picks up small objects with pincer grasp.
Will hold a pencil and scribble and may be using preferred hand most of the time.
May have bowel control and begin to show an interest in potty.
Feeds self with a spoon and gets most of the food into the mouth.
Tries to undress – attempts to unfasten shoe and pulls off socks.

Intellectual development

Very curious and determined to explore the environment with increasing understanding of where things belong.
Enjoys putting objects into containers and then tipping them out again.
Likes books with pictures of everyday objects in them and helps turn the pages, several at a time.
Imitates simple everyday activities, like driving the car, using a telephone.
Can build a tower of three bricks or other everyday objects, like cushions, cardboard boxes.
Can point to several parts of the body – nose, eyes, ears, etc.

Language development

Chatters continuously while playing.
Uses 6–20+ words but understands many more.
Enjoys rhymes and tries to join in.
Attempts to sing and often seems to recognize TV themes.
Obeys simple requests, e.g. go and get grandma's car keys.

Social development

Plays quite well by herself but likes to be near a familiar adult or older brother or sister.
Plays alongside other children and seems to enjoy their company but does not play *with* them.

Enjoys songs, rhymes and books with adults (enjoys the individual attention).

Emotional development

Very dependent on familiar adult but likes to be independent at times, and this can cause conflict.
Loves cuddles, fun games, tickling, hiding, chasing.

Two years old

At 2 years of age children take an enormous step forward in their intellectual development. They are learning to construct simple sentences, which will be the basis on which they will develop verbal fluency in the third and fourth year. The child is still very curious, restless and enjoys a great deal of motor activity but may be able to sustain very short periods of concentrated effort on an activity.

Physical development

Runs safely and is more efficient at avoiding obstacles.
Loves to climb over the furniture.
Walks up and down stairs – two feet to a stair.
Pushes and pulls large wheeled toys with a growing sense of which direction she wants them to go.
Throws a ball overhead and kicks it.
Sits on small tricycle but uses feet not pedals to move it.
Holds pencil in preferred hand using thumb and first two fingers.
Scribbles circles and dots and imitates a vertical line with practice.
Spoon-feeds, drinks and chews efficiently.
Usually has control of bowels and may be dry in the daytime.
Will have cut or will soon cut last tooth.
Puts on socks and shoes (not necessarily on right foot).

Intellectual development

Enjoys picture books and recognizes smaller details – turns pages more slowly.
Very curious about surroundings but has little understanding of common dangers.
Has no understanding of the need to defer immediate wishes – can't wait!
Engages in simple role or make-believe play.

Builds a tower of six or seven blocks.
Can point to parts of body including knees, elbows, etc.

Language development

Speech more recognizable.
Uses 50+ words and understands many more.
Puts two or more words together to form a sentence.
Beginning to listen with interest to talk going on around and responds to conversations directed towards them.
Refers to self by name and talks continually during play.
Constantly asks the name of objects and people in order to learn new words.
Joins in familiar rhymes and songs which they love to have repeated – a favourite word is 'again'.
Carries out instructions – when feels like it!

Social development

Follows carer around the house and imitates, constantly demanding attention.
Likes a response from an adult when has done something.
Plays contentedly near other children but not with them – parallel play.
Has no idea about sharing playthings or the adult's attention and will hold on to own possessions with determination.

Emotional development

Still in need of much attention, reassurance and love.
Very dependent on adults and jealous of attention given to others.
Can be loving one minute and biting the next.

Two-and-a-half years

At $2\frac{1}{2}$ the child is poised between dependence on a familiar adult and the ability to broaden horizons and spend some time with other adults and children at playschool. Physically quite proficient, and able to be understood verbally most of the time, they often still need the security of a familiar environment and should not be pushed too soon.

Physical development

Locomotor skills improving rapidly with practice.
Walks upstairs easily and downstairs, two feet to a step.

Runs well and stops efficiently, usually avoiding obstacles.
Climbs nursery and garden apparatus, but may get stuck at the top.
Can jump with two feet together from a low step.
Throws and kicks a ball with some idea of where it will go.
Eats skilfully with hands and utensils.
Pulls down pants to use the toilet but needs assistance to pull them up.
Usually dry in the day and maybe at night (very variable).

Intellectual development

Still little understanding of everyday dangers or the need to wait for something – including attention.
Builds a tower of 7+ blocks.
Enjoys picture books with minute detail in them.
Holds a chubby pencil and will copy a horizontal line and circle.
Recognizes self in a photograph and knows own full name.
More sustained role play – from life and TV characters.
Plays meaningfully with miniature toys, e.g. farm animals and plastic cartoon characters, adding own commentary to the story.

Language development

Uses 200 or more recognizable words.
Continually asking 'what?', 'who?'.
Uses 'I', 'me', and 'you' correctly in conversation.
Says a few nursery rhymes – more with the prompting of an adult.

Social development

Watches other children at play, occasionally joining in for a few minutes but not really interested in sharing a game. Very happy to play with adults or older children who will give undivided attention and let the child win.

Emotional development

Still very dependent on adult.
Throws tantrum when thwarted and is less easily distracted.

Three years old

The 3-year-old is more agile and co-ordinated. Language is becoming an increasingly important tool – its social use is developing and if language development is retarded the child may find it difficult to make friends, join in group activities or obey fairly complicated instructions from an adult. All these things are necessary when the child begins to move out of the family circle and start playgroup, which is usual at this age. If the child is not able to use or understand language then anti-social behaviour may persist.

Physical development

Can jump with feet together, stand and walk on tiptoe and stand on one leg.
Uses climbing frames well.
Can steer round obstacles and corners while running and pushing toys.
Walks upstairs with alternating feet but still two feet to the stair coming down.
With practice, can ride a tricycle or bicycle with stabilizers (see Figure 7.7), kick a ball forcibly and hold and cut with scissors.
Can use a spoon and fork to eat if this is the family practice.
May be dry at night but not unusual if not (especially boys).
Can pull pants up and down.
Needs help with buttons when dressing.
Washes hands but needs help drying.
Able to use technical equipment like computers if allowed.

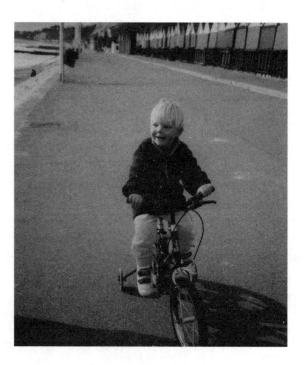

Figure 7.7 Three years old: with practice, can ride a bicycle with stabilizers.

Intellectual development

Shows some appreciation of difference between present and past and the need to wait for attention, sweets, ride on the swings, etc. (This is not highly developed and the 3-year-old will still have difficulty understanding the need to take turns.)
Builds a tower of nine bricks and copies a bridge made with them.
Enjoys floor play with bricks, boxes, etc. which can be used imaginatively.
Copies O, V and T shapes.

Draws a person with head and usually some indication of one or two features.
Matches colours and may name two or three.
Enjoys painting for the sake of it with fingers or brush.
Plays inventive, imaginative games with make-believe people and objects.
Can count up to ten or more but has little appreciation of actual quantity beyond two or three.
Listens quietly to stories and loves to hear them over again.
Knows several rhymes and songs.
Can tell you full name and sex.

Language development

Extensive vocabulary which is usually intelligible even to strangers.
Uses pronouns and plurals but may overgeneralize, e.g. 'sheeps'.
Initiates simple conversations by asking many questions: 'who?', 'why?', 'what?', 'where?'
Speech beginning to gain interest by changes of tone in the sentence.

Social development

General behaviour more co-operative – likes to help adults with activities.
Begins to join in games with other children and to share but still needs to be in a small group.

Emotional development

Much steadier emotionally and so easier to manage.
Emotional maturity shows in friendliness, sociability and desire to please.

Affectionate towards carers, brothers and sisters and pets.

Feels more secure, so is able to share and play with others (this can revert if the child is unwell or feels less sure – e.g. new surroundings or unfamiliar adults).

Four years old

After a period of emotional and developmental stability, around 3 years, children are again showing a 'see-saw' pattern of behaviour at the age of 4. In struggling for the verbal, social and emotional confidence of the 5-year-old the 4-year-old can become 'a boastful, dogmatic and bossy showoff'. Their minds are lively, their imagination vivid and their will strong, but their emotional unsteadiness shows itself in verbal impertinence and exaggeration.

Physical development

Very agile: can turn sharp corners when running, hop, tiptoe, climb trees and ladders.

Climbs stairs and descends confidently one foot to a stair.

Expert tricycle rider, using pedals and avoiding obstacles.

Increased skill in ball games – throws, catches, bounces and kicks with an idea of where the ball is going.

Good control of pencil, which is held adult fashion.

Able to thread small beads onto a string and use scissors with practice.

Capable of washing and drying hands but often in too much of a hurry to complete the job well.

Can dress and undress except laces, ties and back buttons.

Intellectual development

Has an understanding of past, present and future time.

Builds tower of 10+ bricks and bridge. Can copy steps built of bricks.

Floor games very complicated, and construction play utilizes any available material.

Dramatic make-believe play can be sustained for long periods.

Copies cross, square and VHTO shapes.

Draws a recognizable house and a person with head, possible trunk, legs and arms.

Beginning to name drawings and plan models before starting them.

Matches and names four colours correctly.

Recognizes and names circle, square and triangle.

Gives full name, address and age.

Able to recount recent events.

Sometimes confuses fact and fantasy but able to relate long stories. Enjoys jokes.

Counts by rote up to 20 or more and may have understanding of number to four or five.

Enjoys learning new skills like computer games.

Language development

Speech intelligible and essentially grammatically correct.

May still have difficulty pronouncing w – f – th.

Continually asking questions: 'why?', 'when?', 'how?'

Loves new words and will invent them in order to tell a story or put an unknown into context, e.g. a picture of a camel is described as a 'horse with a hump'.

Social development

Likes the companionship of other children and adults but alternates between co-operation and conflict.

However, understands the need to use words rather than blows.

Capable of sharing and taking turns but may cheat in order to win – this is very obvious in games like Snakes and Ladders.

Shows sympathy for friends who are hurt.

Emotional development

Is in a period of emotional unsteadiness, which is shown by cheekiness and impertinence rather than temper tantrums.

General behaviour more independent and self-willed, which can lead to conflict.

Five years old

If raised in the right environment 5-year-olds are confident and have good self-control. Home will no longer satisfy their curiosity and desire for knowledge, and they are ready for the wider experience of school. Having achieved a measure of independence they are able to cope with the larger group and no longer require to have so much adult attention – although they will always thrive on praise and be proud of their achievements.

Physical development

Movements precise: runs lightly on toes and is able to walk along narrow line.
Skilful in climbing, swinging and sliding.
Able to skip, hop and move rhythmically to music.
Kicks and throws ball with considerable ability by focusing eyes on the objective.
Good control of pencil, crayons and paint brushes.
Able to thread a large needle and sew stitches.
Well-developed IT skills – video, computer.
Uses a knife and fork with practice.
Washes and dries face and hands, and can dress and undress (may need help with laces and ties).

Intellectual development

Draws recognizable people with head, trunk, features, arms and legs.
Creates pictures – usually of people, houses, flowers and a large sun in the sky.
Decides what to draw before commencing – although will often look across at neighbour and include something that they have drawn!
Beginning to distinguish between truth and falsehood.
Enjoys games with rules. May still attempt to 'cheat to win' but has an awareness of 'not fair'.
Capable of colouring neatly and staying within the line.
Names at least four colours.
Can name and draw circle, square, rectangle and triangle.
Writes a few letters – can often write own name in capital letters.
Counts fingers on one hand with the index finger of the other.
Loves to be read or told stories, which will often be acted out later in complicated dramatic play.
Shows a definite sense of humour and loves telling 'jokes'.
Understands the *need* for tidiness but requires constant reminders to *be* tidy.
Realizes clock time has a relationship to the daily routine of events.

Language development

Speech fluent and grammatically correct.
Loves new words and learns songs quickly.
Constantly asks meaning of new words.
Recognizes some written words and begins to write a few.

Social development

Ready to mix with a wider group and to choose friends.
Proud of achievements and possessions.
Co-operative with friends most of the time and understands the need for rules.
Protective towards younger children and pets and shows concern if they are upset.

Emotional development

Generally more sensible and controlled.
Independent and ready to cope with challenges but needs praise and encouragement in order to progress.

Six years old

Physically children continue to mature and refine their control of movement. Growth rate slows down. Emotionally the child is entering another period of upheaval. Between the ages of 5 and 7 there is a major change in the way children think and feel and the 6-year-old may experience difficulties in maintaining balance in their emotional behaviour. There are often swings of mood, periods of frenzied activity, and nightmares are not unusual. However, we can harness these energies by interesting children in new ideas and objects and encouraging them to explore and learn.

Physical development

Constantly 'on the go'. Rush about and often slam into things. However, the body is well co-ordinated, and eye and hand work together so that bat and ball games are more successful.
Girls and boys are equally boisterous, but the energies are often channelled into cartwheels and dance for the girls, and wrestling for the boys. Boys will often 'play' fighting – this can end in tears as they do not know when to stop. There will of course be cultural and social differences which will shape how boys and girls are expected to act.
All this dashing about makes children tired but they hate to give in and rest.
The child is beginning to lose first teeth as the second ones come through.

Intellectual development

Easily distracted because of physical energy, so learning is best channelled into exploratory methods where possible. The mind is very active
and the child will move easily from one activity to another, but the 6-
year-old will complete a task on another day. Decisions are not made as
quickly as before, as more thinking is required – this shows increased
maturity in weighing up the possibilities.
Draws more realistic and complicated pictures and begins to fill in the
colour.
Interested in learning to read, as loves stories.
Learning to write but may still reverse some letters.
Has a better understanding of number symbols and enjoys games like
dominoes.

Language development

The 6-year-old is an incessant chatterer so enjoys oral work, but language
now widens to include reading, writing and tapes, etc. There has been a
great deal of research undertaken into the best method of teaching children to read. There does not appear to be any easy answer, but it can
only be a help if we surround the child with all forms of language and
demonstrate a love of it ourselves.

Social development

A difficult period as friendships form and dissolve rapidly. The child
often plays better with one rather than two friends. Although not always
the case, boys are more likely to fight and girls to use verbal taunts when
they fall out: 'You're not coming to my party' is commonly heard.
Children love parties and social functions at this age but it can be a trau-
matic time.
The 6-year-old is eager for praise and recognition and would always like
to win. Attention from teacher/parent will spur him on but he sometimes finds correction difficult to accept.

Emotional development

Because of the increased mental ability, children are able to see that
there are many sides to a question. This can make them hesitant, inde-
cisive and frightened. The 6-year-old is therefore very dependent on
adults for direction and guidance. The stress often shows as nightmares,
which can be very frightening.

The 6-year-old is also capable of bouts of strong verbal and physical temper, but can also be very caring and considerate.

Seven years old

The 7-year-old is a clearer thinker and a steadier personality capable of long periods of concentrated effort. However, the child is moving from the pre-operational way of thinking into the concrete operational. This means that they are able to categorize in various ways which may lead to confusion at times.

Physical development

Less likely to rush about.
Will practise something many times in order to perfect the movement.
Good co-ordination means that they are better at bat and ball games.

Intellectual development

Now in the concrete operational stage which allows them to store, retrieve and reorganize experiences to fit them to new challenges.
Because they have an insight into conclusions they often rub out their work in an attempt to be 'right'.
Enjoy experimenting and manipulating with new materials. Able to tell the time well.

Language development

Uses language much more to reason, but still shouts if thinks something is unfair.
Enjoys exciting stories being read to them, but also reads to self more.
Likes books with strong heroes.
Interested in words – likes poetry.
Able to write stories for self.

Social development

Very self-aware – no longer likes to get changed with other children.
Becoming more aware of the needs and feelings of others and likes to help.
Moving away from dependence on family for reassurance – anxious to please the teacher and older friends.
Has a gang of friends – ready to join clubs.

Emotional development

Personality quite well established.
Still not a good loser.
Absorbs more than gives out, so appears quieter.
Has a growing sense of right and wrong.
Outbursts are rarer – more likely to sulk if upset.
Because of increased ability to imagine what is likely to occur, may have fears about self in new situations. This can cause problems with the move to a new school.

References

Brain, J. and Martin, M. (1989) *Childcare and Health for Nursery Nurses*, (3rd edn). Cheltenham: Thorne.

Fishbein, H. (1984) *The Psychology of Infancy and Childhood: Evolutionary and Cross-cultural Perspectives*. Hillsdale, NJ: Erlbaum.

Geraghty, P. (1988) *Caring for Children* (2nd edn). London: Baillière Tindall.

Grieve, R. and Hughes, M. (eds) (1990) *Understanding Children*. Oxford: Blackwell.

Lee, C. (1990) *The Growth and Development of Children* (4th edn). Harlow: Longman.

Ott, P. (1997) *How to Detect and Manage Dyslexia*. London: Heinemann.

Piaget, J. (1926) *The Language and Thought of the Child*. New York: Harcourt, Brace.

Reynolds, V. (1994) *A Practical Guide to Child Development*, vol. 1: *The Child*. Cheltenham: Thorne.

Sheridan, M. (1995) *The Developmental Progress of Infants and Young Children* (3rd edn). London: HMSO.

Sheridan, M. (1980) *From Birth to Five Years*. London: NFER.

Tough, J. (1976) *Listening to Children Talking*. London: Ward Lock Education.

DfEE with SCAA (1996) *Nursery Education: Desirable Outcomes for Children's Learning on Entering Compulsory Education*. London: DfEE and SCAA.

Hants C.C. (1998) Hampshire Guidelines (1998): *Early Years Plan and Partnership: Learning Together from the Beginning*. Hants County Council.

Surrey Early Years Guidelines (1998): Children First. Surrey County Council.

Further Reading

Bee, H. (1992) *The Developing Child*. London: HarperCollins.

Davenport, G. (1988) *An Introduction to Child Development*. London: Unwin Hyman.

Hobart, C. and Frankel, J. (1992) *A Practical Guide to Working with Young Children*. Cheltenham: Thorne.

Laishley, J. (1987) *Working with Young Children*. Sevenoaks, Kent: Arnold.

Lindon, J. (ed.) (1993) *Child Development from Birth–Eight: A Practical Focus*. London: National Children's Bureau.

Matteson, E. M. (1989) *Play with a Purpose for the Under Sevens*. London: Penguin.

Meadows, S. (1986) *Understanding Child Development*. London: Routledge.

Smith, G. and Gowrie, H. (1988) *Understanding Children's Development*. Oxford: Blackwell.

Index